THE UNSTUDIED CURRICULUM:

ITS IMPACT ON CHILDREN

By the ASCD Elementary Education Council

Edited by Norman V. Overly

Association for Supervision and Curriculum Development, NEA
1201 Sixteenth Street, N.W., Washington, D.C. 20036

Copyright © 1970 by the
Association for Supervision and Curriculum Development, NEA

All rights reserved. No part of this publication may be reproduced or transmitted in any form or by any means, electronic or mechanical, including photocopy, recording, or any information storage and retrieval system, without permission in writing from the publisher.

Price: $2.75

NEA Stock Number: 611-17820

The materials printed herein are the expressions of the writers and not a statement of policy of the Association unless set by resolution.

Library of Congress Catalog Card Number: 70-119590

Contents

Acknowledgments	iv
Foreword John D. Greene	v
Preface Norman V. Overly	vi
Introduction Philip W. Jackson	ix
The Consequences of Schooling Philip W. Jackson	1
Curriculum as Educational Process: The Middle Class Against Itself Edgar Z. Friedenberg	16
The Impact of School Philosophy and Practice on Child Development Barbara Biber, Patricia Minuchin	27
Teacher Expectation and Pupil Learning Robert Rosenthal	53
Schooling and Authority: Comments on the Unstudied Curriculum Robert Dreeben	85
The Moral Atmosphere of the School Lawrence Kohlberg	104
Contributors	128
Members of the ASCD Elementary Education Council	129
Conference Staff	130

Acknowledgments

FINAL editing of the manuscript and production of this booklet were the responsibility of Robert R. Leeper, Associate Secretary and Editor, ASCD Publications. Technical production was handled by Mary Albert O'Neill, Lana G. Pipes, Nancy Olson, and Karen T. Brakke. Cover and title page were designed by Robert J. McMeans, NEA Publications Division.

Foreword

ISSUANCE of this paperbound booklet by the Association for Supervision and Curriculum Development is entirely appropriate. The significance of the area of instruction, of curriculum, for members of ASCD is indicated by the presence of the world "curriculum" in our organization's title. In this publication the focus is on the *unstudied* part of the curriculum, upon the affective, the internalized, the invisible but indelibly etched learnings of children who are "experiencing and undergoing" education.

This organization is recognized for its belief that humanness, or humaneness, should be respected in and enhanced through the curriculum. Each author in this booklet has sharpened our insights through his unique presentation.

A great deal of the work of the Association for Supervision and Curriculum Development is accomplished through the deliberations and projects of its councils, commissions, and committees. This publication exemplifies one part of the outstanding work of the ASCD Elementary Education Council.

ASCD collaborates with other organizations when there is mutual concern. The American Association of Elementary-Kindergarten-Nursery Educators shared in this conference on "The Unstudied Curriculum: Its Impact on Children." Its members will find much of reward and interest in this booklet, which includes the papers presented during this jointly sponsored conference.

ASCD is most grateful to the scholars who presented these papers, and to the participants at the meeting. Their eager interest in the topic of the conference reassured us of the timeliness and significance of this attempt to assess the "unstudied curriculum."

> JOHN D. GREENE, *President 1970-71*
> *Association for Supervision*
> *and Curriculum Development*

Preface

THE papers included in this publication were originally developed and presented at the Third Annual Elementary Conference sponsored by the Elementary Education Council of the Association for Supervision and Curriculum Development in cooperation with E/K/N/E. The conference was held January 8-11, 1969, in Washington, D.C.

From the initial planning stages the Council gave attention to a wide range of concerns related to "conferencing." What are the possibilities of the conference format? Should a conference primarily inform? Does a conference have any impact beyond the participants? Given the diverse set of expectations and assumptions brought by participants, are common outcomes possible and/or desirable? How can one maximize the effectiveness of a conference?

High on the list of concerns of the organizers of this meeting was that of providing opportunity for involvement in the proceedings by as many individuals as possible. To this end a format of formal presentation of papers followed by small group discussions and interchange with the authors was established. In addition participants were requested to respond to a post-conference questionnaire inquiring about follow-up activities which grew out of conference experiences. Furthermore it was decided to prepare the papers for publication as another avenue for dissemination of the proceedings. This publication is the result.

The theme of the conference was very broad. The planners in no way intended that the proceedings serve as a definitive statement on all aspects of the "unstudied curriculum." Perhaps the papers, follow-up activities, personal reflections on the meetings, and this booklet will serve to awaken some readers to the multifaceted splendor of the learning process and the complexity of the teaching task. Perhaps these experiences will have extended the impact of the conference beyond the conferees and will have accomplished at least a portion of our wider objective.

It should be noted that two of the speakers at the conference are not represented by papers in this volume. Their charge was to bring reactions to the earlier presentations to the final session and to indicate what they considered to be primary implications of the unstudied curriculum for current practice and the formal, studied curriculum. Mr. Kenneth Haskins, at that time Principal of the Morgan Community School, Washington, D.C., and Dr. Dwayne Huebner, Professor of Education, Teachers College, Columbia University, performed this service through a dialogue including other conference participants.

The theme of the conference, "The Unstudied Curriculum: Its Impact on Children," reflects not only an area of concern by the group of scholars represented here. As Haskins and Huebner made clear, this theme serves to focus attention on an aspect of education which is gaining headlines almost daily as the public increasingly asks or demands to know what is happening to children. It is no longer enough lamely to indicate that Jane is not performing up to grade level or that Jim is weak in math. Parents want to know why and they want to know in specifics why the schools are not helping their children more. Furthermore, they suspect that there is an important relationship between the hidden, unstudied, informal, unexpected, subsidiary, or concomitant learnings and the planned, structured, studied, or formal programs of the educational establishment.

During the final session Kenneth Haskins made this point most sharply:

> There was a lot of talk here about research. Someone mentioned that Ken Clark had said something about the ghetto. Whatever he said, I was familiar with it. Not only Ken Clark said it, my mother said it, my father said it, and a lot of people have been saying it for a lot of years. If you look at the whole movement for community control, you will see that what parents and what other people are talking about is really what we [at this conference] are talking about. They are not talking about teachers not knowing math or not knowing science. They are saying that the teachers do not have the right attitudes about *my* children or that the teachers do not believe *my* children can learn. I want a teacher in the school who treats me and my children with dignity and respect.

Obviously, this compilation of ideas, research reports, and

personal perspective is insufficient to meet the challenges to education. What is needed is personal commitment and involvement by each educator. As Haskins noted, schools need not solve all the problems of society, but they should not contribute to them. Part of not contributing to problems is being aware of them. Huebner suggested several "awarenesses" each educator should develop. For example, we should be more aware of the history of curriculum development. Much that we treat as new today has been considered before, albeit under different names. We need to be aware of the "racist" nature of our society, our institutions, and our personal perspectives. We need to be aware of the control exercised over our society by the military-industrial-academic complex.

It is not possible to reconstruct in a brief introduction the setting and feelings that surrounded the conference itself. This booklet will require of each reader an attempt at openness and receptivity to the ideas expressed and a commitment to involve himself in the educative task of translating the printed word into meaningful action. A major part of the message for the reader may lie between the lines.

March 1970   NORMAN V. OVERLY
*ASCD Associate Secretary
and Liaison Staff Member,
ASCD Elementary Education Council*

Introduction

THE assertion that school attendance typically results in more than the acquisition of a set of academic skills or knowledge is hardly controversial enough to raise a single eyebrow among today's educators. Everyone, or certainly everyone who has given the matter any thought, will readily acknowledge that a student's progress in reading, writing, arithmetic, and other subdivisions of the curriculum tells only part of the story of what school has done to and for him. In addition to his growth in these conventional terms, there are alterations in attitudes, motives, values, and other psychological states that bear a complicated relationship to the experiences he has had in the classroom. Indeed, some would argue that these nonacademic outcomes of formal education are often of greater consequence for the student's ultimate well-being than are those changes commonly thought to be the main business of instruction.

If, in the process of becoming familiar with the works of Shakespeare, a student develops a conviction that the Bard was insufferably dull, his teacher might well begin to wonder whether the total effort was worthwhile. If a child's early encounters with reading instruction weaken his desire to master that important skill, surely he has lost more than he has gained, no matter what his scores on a reading readiness test tell us. And what are we to conclude about the overall effect of schooling if, long after the grit of chalk dust has been washed from our pores, we look back on our experience with the sad conviction of someone like George Orwell, who once observed,

When I was fourteen or fifteen I was an odious little snob, but no worse than other boys of my own age and class. I suppose there is no place in the world where snobbery is quite so ever-present or where it is cultivated in such refined and subtle forms as in an English public school. Here at least one cannot say that English "education" fails to do its job. You forget your Latin and Greek within a few months of leaving school—I studied Greek for eight or ten years, and now, at thirty-three, I cannot even repeat the Greek alphabet—but your snobbishness, unless you persistently root it out like the bindweed it is, sticks by you till your grave.[1]

Fortunately, not all of these by-products of schooling are undesirable, though the examples I have used might give that impression. Sometimes a student's initial contact with the works of Shakespeare is but the start of a lifelong interest in serious literature. Often a child's beginning struggles with reading not only sharpen his desire to learn more but also leave him convinced of the importance of all that goes on in his classroom. Some of us, even on distant reflection, can attribute to our experience in school ways of looking at the world, which, though not directly related to the material we were taught, are yet among the most valuable consequences of our having been there.

Given the obvious importance of changes such as these, it is puzzling to find them being referred to in some quarters as mere "side effects" or "incidental outcomes" of instruction and, consequently, treated quite casually or overlooked completely in discussions of our educational priorities. One would think that such matters, regardless of the labels attached to them, would be taken more seriously than they typically are by all who are interested in education.

One reason for this apparent neglect is that we seem to have so little control over these phenomena. No matter how hard teachers try, some students wind up as educational casualties in more than just the academic sense. Others, also quite inexplicably, remain buoyant and spirited almost despite what happens to them in the classroom. These circumstances possibly explain why many educational leaders prefer to turn their attention to less capricious processes, leaving the classroom teacher to cope as best she can with what look to be will-o-the-wisp events. Nor is it surprising to find that one of the most popular strategies for the day-to-day coping with these unpredictable happenings is for the teacher to cross her fingers, smile, and plunge ahead with Dick and Jane.

Although a conference such as the one for which these papers were prepared cannot be expected to redress the imbalance of our educational concerns, it is, we believe, a sign that a change of perspective may be in the offing. An increasing number of people, both inside and outside the ranks of professional educators, are beginning to study the total process of schooling—what it does to

---

[1] George Orwell. *The Road to Wigan Pier.* Baltimore: Penguin Books, Inc., 1962. p. 120.

people and how it achieves its effects. As a result of such study some investigators have become severe critics of our schools and of those who work in them. Others, though they may hold strong private opinions about what the schools should do, are content to present their findings in a more neutral spirit, leaving it to the practitioner to derive whatever implications he sees fit.

The papers that follow were prepared by educators and social scientists representing several positions along the continuum extending from impassioned critic of education to seemingly neutral observer. To the best of my knowledge, these presentations do not include staunch defenders of the status quo, though perhaps that conservative position will be voiced by some of our readers after they have examined what a few of the writers have to say.

The developers of these papers hope each reader will take time to discuss and reflect upon what is written here, just as those who heard the papers did at the time of their initial presentation. Given the state of our knowledge, or perhaps I should say our ignorance, such contemplation is essential. In short, these papers do not try to set forth "the word" from the experts, though what the authors have to say will certainly provide the starting point for many discussions. Rather, an attempt is made here to expose an important aspect of education, one that strikes us as being sufficiently unexplored to warrant the label we have assigned it: the unstudied curriculum.

PHILIP W. JACKSON, *Chairman*
ASCD Elementary Education Council

The Consequences of Schooling

Philip W. Jackson

Like most other participants in this conference, I too have been trying to understand what happens to people as a result of their experiences in classrooms. My efforts, in themselves, may not entitle me to take up more of your time than I already have, but since it hardly seems worthwhile to have traveled all the way from England* to say what I have just said, I feel compelled to continue. I do believe the remarks I shall make, stemming as they do from my observations in classrooms, are directly related to the theme of this conference, though I suspect they may do more to stir up dust than to settle the air. Indeed, the very act of giving voice to them has convinced me that I need to know a lot more than I presently do about some of the issues over which philosophers have been arguing for quite a time. My ignorance of these matters, however, is probably no greater than that of most other non-philosophers who are engaged in various aspects of education. This rather dubious consolation, plus the fact that I felt obliged to justify my transatlantic flight, has given me sufficient courage to plunge ahead, dust or no dust.

External Evidence

Often when I walk past an elementary school late in the day, after the children have gone home and before the janitor has completed his work, my eye is caught by the inevitable pieces of debris the departing students have left in their wake. There, mingling with the dead leaves that swirl in circles in the play yard, are scraps from some secret message that likely was passed surreptitiously

*At the time of presentation of this paper, Dr. Jackson was spending a year writing and studying in England.

2 THE UNSTUDIED CURRICULUM: ITS IMPACT ON CHILDREN

from hand to hand in the closing minutes before dismissal. High in a tree, where the wind has taken it, is a permission slip that will never be delivered and the first page of a homework assignment that will have to be redone. In the gutter, near where the buses were parked, lies a brightly-colored painting by Kathy B. whose signature, printed in dripping red in the upper right-hand corner, is now barely discernible beneath the black impression of a tire track. Occasionally, whole composition books and even bulkier objects are to be found among this flotsam and jetsam, leading me to wonder what their former owners will do when they discover their loss. Here, in concrete terms, are some of the things we leave behind when our schooling is finished.

But what of the things we take with us? What do *they* look like? In asking such a question we are forced to broaden the scope of our thinking to include much more than a mere catalogue of physical products, for the crayon drawings and the spelling lists and the lecture notes—even those that finally reach home—are of little consequence when compared to the invisible changes that have taken place inside each student. Obviously, if we want to come to grips with what school does to people, we must not allow ourselves to be distracted by the easily observable but, instead, must seek to understand phenomena that can never be seen. Yet one important similarity between these "inside" and "outside" products bears mention before we move on.

Internal Evidence

Internally as well as externally we have a way of losing things. The litter in the schoolyard has its parallel in the psychic stuff that has escaped the net of memory, never to be retrieved. Inside our skins, as well as outside, messages can be blown adrift. Indeed, the extent of this internal loss, if we could ever estimate its amount, might well make the junk in the janitor's canvas sack look small in comparison.

To understand how this might be so, we need to recognize that the most immediate and direct effects of schooling reside in our memory of our classroom experience as it happened, minute by minute, hour by hour, day by day. In fact, this memorial residue is so intimately linked to the experience itself that I shall refer to it as the *primary* consequence of schooling and shall call all other consequences *secondary*. This designation is not intended to imply that a student's memory of what happened in school is more important than other changes that might have taken place, only that it is more easily traced to actual classroom events than are other types of consequence.

Primary Consequences of Schooling

As we think of the vast number of events that can be crowded into a person's life each day, whether he spends it inside or outside a classroom, we can hardly be surprised to discover that his impressions of all he has experienced behave like the photographer's proofs that quickly darken on exposure to light, leaving only the shadowy traces of images that were once bright and clear. Nor is it simply the magnitude of experience that makes this process understandable. Most of what we witness each day seems to have such fleeting significance for our lives that a highly detailed and enduring memory of it would seem to serve no purpose and might even be thought of as burdensome. In addition, if we consider the possibility of there being a genuine limit to the capacity of our memory storage, with the attendant danger of filling our mental trunks with useless baggage, so to speak, the adaptive significance of rapid memory loss begins to look even more like a blessing in disguise.

Small wonder then that, by the time he reaches home in the afternoon, the student's images of school life that he carries with him have already faded to the point of being hardly more than pale reminders of what life was like that day. Also, like the snapshots brought back by a traveler to a foreign land, the student's memories, even those that stay with him for some time, not only are small in comparison to all that happened to him but represent a highly select sample from the hodgepodge of the total experience. The size and selectivity of this sample will become important when we turn to some of the secondary consequences of schooling. For the moment we only need pause to mention a few of the principles under which the selection process likely operates.

Principles of Mental Operations

We might begin by reminding ourselves of some of the things that are known in general about the working of human memory. We know, for example, that our memories tend to be structured in much the same way that our perceptions are structured. That is, we remember things, people, and events rather than the minute sensations of which these complex entities seem to be composed.

Indeed, our tendency to see and to remember whole objects and to make sense of what we see is so strong that we sometimes distort reality by filling in missing parts in our mind's eye or overlooking slight irregularities and anomalies. If, however, what we see is too unusual, the very fact of its novelty increases the likelihood that we will spend more time perceiving it and, hence, remember it longer.

Our memory of people and their actions seems to entail a special set of operating principles. It is influenced, for example, by the social attributes of status and authority. Because of their greater power to influence our lives, some of the people with whom we have contact are more salient to us than are others. Thus, we tend to recall our encounters with them more clearly than we do similar encounters with people whose actions are less intimately related to our well-being. This self-centeredness of our perception and memory is also reflected in the fact that, other things being equal, we retain a sharper image of those actions in which we were a participant and particularly those in which our feelings were aroused than we do those events of which we were merely passive and detached observers.

These few principles of mental operation are sufficient to provide a rough indication of how a child's memory of his school experience might assume the shape it has by the time his parents query him at the supper table. Even if we assume that he will tell them all he remembers (a dangerous assumption, indeed!), it is safe to bet that his report will emphasize *unusual* events: the things his teacher said and did; the things that happened to him, his friends, and other "significant" people; and those aspects of his experience that were particularly satisfying or discomforting. By the time he has finished, his parents may join him in believing he has told all that happened in school that day. But of course he has not.

Yet even acknowledging that a lot has been left out, they may still want to believe him when he insists on his having related all the *important* happenings of the day. However, by so believing they commit the mistake of treating events as important or unimportant solely on the basis of whether they are or are not remembered. Clearly such a practice places too much reliance on the perfection and omniscience of the human mind. Some aspects of our experience must surely be important from certain points of view yet not registered in our memory or perhaps never even fully perceived. The likelihood of this state of affairs should prevent parents, and teachers as well, from relying too heavily on a student's memory as a guide to all the important events that transpire in classrooms.

Accuracy and Completeness of Memory

Yet even though we might wish to question its accuracy and completeness, the memorial residue of a student's schooling is worth pondering a bit longer if only to raise a question or two about the relationship between mental phenomena in general and academic learning in particular. If we became too absorbed in tracing the intricacies of this relationship we would soon find ourselves, I fear, in regions where it is unsafe to travel without a professional philosopher as a guide. I shall try to skirt this epistemological jungle at a respectful distance while pointing out just a few of the flora and fauna that live on its edge.

Consider, first, a student's response to that classic parental query: "What did you learn in school today, dear?" How does he construct a truthful answer? Presumably by reviewing, in some mysterious way, his memory of what happened that day and reporting on a portion of it. This process reveals that many of the things we commonly think of as having learned, particularly those bits of knowledge and skills that are often referred to as "school learning," are originally lodged in our memory as part of the primary consequence of having been in the classroom. To say we "learned" these things is equivalent to saying we remember them. Thus the student can report that he learned that Columbus discovered America because he remembers his teacher having said so. His newly acquired ability to form a capital "B" is intimately connected with his memory of seeing how the teacher did it at the blackboard.

Through repeated exposure and use, these bits of knowledge and skill become separated from their situational context, with the result that today I still know Columbus discovered America even though I cannot remember the exact circumstances under which I learned it. Incidentally, it is interesting to note that we often comment with some regret on the loss of this situational specificity. Thus, in conversations we often catch ourselves and others saying things like "I can't remember where I read it but . . ." or "I heard somewhere that . . ." There was a time, of course, shortly after the event itself, when we could have remembered where we had read or heard what we now know.

In addition to the remembered facts and skills that would satisfy a parent's demand for evidence of something called "learning," there exists among the residue of the student's experience a broad class of memories of quite a different kind. These memories also involve knowledge of a sort but, curiously enough, they are seldom attended to by those of us responsible for a student's formal instruction. Among the bits of knowing included in this class are items of obvious social utility, such as knowing the names of one's classmates, or remembering where one's desk is located, as well as items that seem to be worthless or trivial, such as knowing there is a crack in the window next to the radiator or knowing there are thirteen pieces of petrified chewing gum stuck to the bottom of one's desk.

There is also a great deal of this "knowledge" that is not easy to classify on the basis of its utility or lack of it, such as knowing where the principal's office is located or knowing that your classmate received a higher grade in arithmetic than you did. But regardless of its utility and no matter whether or not we dignify it by calling it "knowledge," this is part and, I would argue, a large part of the residue of schooling. Educators may brush it aside as "incidental" to the main purpose of their work, but this judgment does not alter its reality. Moreover, if we begin to envision what the student's inner world would be like without this seemingly extraneous stuff, its psychological necessity becomes apparent. What if a student did *not* remember the names of any of his classmates or where his desk was located or what his teacher looked like? What if he never attended to any of the trivial details of his environment, like the crack in the window or the lumps of hardened gum under his desk? What if the location of the principal's office, together with the level of his classmate's achievement in arithmetic, remained a mystery to him? If his head were only filled with thoughts of historical facts and scientific principles and timetables, what kind of creature would he be?

"Not human, that's for certain!" is the ready answer. For it is hard to imagine a human being completely lacking in such detailed knowledge. Without it Man would be a perpetual stranger in his environment, a creature blessed with an eternally fresh vision but cursed with the inability ever to feel at home in his surroundings. With it, on the other hand, he comes to know the meaning of the word "familiar" and is free to turn his attention from the concrete and near-at-hand to the abstract and faraway. In a sense then, this extraneous knowledge, or at least some of it, is absolutely essential if a student is ultimately to behave like a student. Further evidence of the importance of such knowledge is reflected in the fact that its acquisition seems to occupy a large part of the student's time during the very first hours following his entry into a classroom.

The practice of organizing an orientation program in some of our larger schools and colleges represents about the only official recognition educators give to the task of helping students acquire a practical acquaintance with their environment. As helpful as such programs might be, they surely do not mark the end of the student's absorption in the nonacademic details of his world. Exactly what function this absorption plays, once a basic orientation and a sense of familiarity have been achieved, no one seems to know. Neither do we know, therefore, the extent to which teachers should concern themselves with such matters. Perhaps they should forget the whole thing and let nature take its course. Yet surely if they are interested in what goes on in students' minds they can't help wondering what to make of these mental odds and ends. I know I can't. Indeed, I suspect that if we knew more about how and why students differ in their awareness of these situational details we could be well on the way toward comprehending many other classroom phenomena.

Secondary Consequences of Schooling

Our understanding of the raw material of classroom memories is further enhanced by turning to the other major category of educational outcomes, that which contains what I have chosen to refer to as the secondary consequences of schooling. These include all those school-related changes that cannot be simply described as the memory of a specific event or an isolated happening. But such a definition by exclusion is obviously too broad to be of much help. In order to arrive at something a little more useful we must move in close enough to identify at least a few of the major subclasses of phenomena covered by our definition. Although this modest step toward greater specificity is obviously insufficient to achieve much clarity, it is all that space limitations will permit.

First, what are here being called the secondary consequences of schooling include all those changes that have something to do with what educators call "academic achievement" while at the same time involving more than the recall of remembered facts and visual images. These secondary consequences comprise such things as a student's awareness of his collective competencies—those sorts of cumulative changes that lead him to say about himself (or others to say about him) things like, "I know how to read," rather than "I know the sound that goes with the letter 'B' " or "I know a lot about the Civil War," as contrasted with "I know the date of Lincoln's assassination."

Second, among these secondary consequences are broad changes in mental functioning that are not directly connected with curricular goals. These include complex intellectual phenomena of which the possessor may have relatively little awareness. They are often discussed under headings such as "cognitive style," "cognitive structure," "mental set," "intelligence," and the like.

Third, and most important within the present context, these secondary consequences include the student's appraisals of himself and of the world in general. These evaluative orientations are connected with dispositions to behave in certain ways and are commonly referred to by a large collection of terms among which are "attitudes," "feelings," "values," "likes and dislikes," "moods," and "tastes."

These three categories obviously represent very gross distinctions within the broad class of secondary consequences. Moreover, the lines separating the three from each other are admittedly quite fuzzy. This separation is adequate, however, for the remainder of my purpose, which is to comment briefly on the overall connection between secondary consequences and educational practices; and then to focus, finally, on that third subclass of secondary changes—those alterations of mood and fancy and attitude and value that are central to the theme of these papers.

Secondary Consequences and Practices

The most important thing to recognize about secondary consequences in general is that, though they may all be school-related, we have no way of knowing exactly to what extent they are school-caused. Moreover, our uncertainty about causes, which was mentioned earlier, is not limited to those changes that involve attitudes and values but extends to the more academic subclasses of these phenomena. Now no one seems to become terribly upset when we suggest that the origin of a child's distaste for school might lie, at least in part, outside his classroom experience. But to hint that his mastery of the three R's might also have taken place outside the protective gaze of his classroom teacher borders on educational heresy.

The suggestion that educators should perhaps share the credit for these intellectual advances with any other institution or set of causal agents would seem to weaken the very foundation on which the case for formal instruction rests. Yet we need only think of activities such as homework and solitary reading and watching television and listening to the radio—not to mention just plain sitting and thinking—to recognize that the school's efforts, even when defined in the narrowest academic terms, are frequently helped or hindered by things students do outside the classroom.

The purpose of calling attention to these outside forces is not to belittle the genuine accomplishments of classroom teachers but, rather, to emphasize the fundamental uncertainty that besets them as they go about their work. A posture of pedagogical faith or courage in the face of this uncertainty requires the teacher to behave almost as if it did not exist. Though he may be pleased or discouraged when the outside world seems to be working with or against him, these feelings, hopefully, will not deter him from acting *as if* he were the only causal agent at work in attaining the benefits he wishes for his students.

Despite the teacher's courage or lack of it, we must continue to seek a deeper understanding of how the home and other environmental influences contribute to what we are here calling the secondary consequences of schooling. Perhaps if we knew more we could do something about changing these influences. But let's not kid ourselves about what such knowledge will do for the classroom teacher. Even if we could demonstrate, for example, that 50 percent of the variance in achievement, unaccounted for by differences in ability, was attributable to the intellectual quality of the home environment, teachers could not, therefore, reduce their efforts by one iota. In short, the people who have charge of our classrooms are paid to do their damndest, no matter what the odds are against their success. No amount of additional knowledge will change that fact.

Evaluative Orientations

We turn now to that third subdivision of secondary consequences, those comprising a wide assortment of what might be called "evaluative orientations"—these are the invisible changes to which we refer when we talk about attitudes, values, likings, tastes, moods, and so forth. Such a varied collection of terms calls for a much more refined analysis than we are prepared to give here. Nonetheless, even without being more precise than this in our definition, several observations can be made about the relationship between these "evaluative orientations" and what takes place in school.

Justification. To begin, we might comment on the linkage, or lack of it, between this type of secondary consequence of schooling and the memorial residue we are calling "primary." Superficially at least, it looks as though there ought to be some kind of match between these two types of consequences, with each attitude or appraisal associated with one or more bits of memory that function in some way like intermediate links in a causal chain. And, indeed, this is the way things often seem to work. Thus, when a student tells us that he dislikes a particular teacher or school subject and we ask him why, he often is able to draw on his memory of past experience to justify his attitude.

Interestingly enough, however, these neat explanatory narratives are not always forthcoming and our queries are often greeted with such unsatisfactory replies as "I don't know why I dislike him," or "There's just something about that subject that turns me off." If we continue to press for an explanation, we sometimes create embarrassment; so we often drop the matter in an effort to be polite, while privately judging the attitude to be unfair because the person holding it seems to have no good reason for doing so. Incidentally, children are more likely to find themselves in these defenseless postures than are adults. By the time we have grown up we avoid confessing most of those attitudes for which we cannot muster a convincing justification.

Yet is it reasonable to expect anyone's memory to serve as an infallible repository of justifying events? I think not, because it implies not only that we are aware of the role that each experience plays in the formation of our attitudes but also that we have total recall of these formative episodes. Neither of these requirements seems to square very well with the facts of mental life as I experience them and as I have come to believe others experience them. I conclude, therefore, that we often must take students at their word when they tell us they like or dislike a teacher or school subject but cannot, at the same time, tell us why they feel the way they do. Moreover, even when students offer an explanation that draws on the details of their experience, the listener would be well-advised to doubt that he has heard the whole causal story. I am not charging that students are a dishonest lot, at least no more so than the rest of us, but only that a convenient matching between the primary and the secondary consequences of schooling is an unreasonable expectation. Commonly, I would argue, people (students included) know *how* they feel about something without knowing *why* they feel the way they do.

This psychological condition has important implications for the way in which we conduct research on classroom affairs. It implies that some of the events that contribute to the formation of attitudes and the like may be too subtle or too minuscule or perhaps even too commonplace to be preserved in the average student's memory of his classroom experience. If this were so, it would mean that our research strategies should be adapted to reveal more of those aspects of classroom life that seem to go unnoticed by the inhabitants themselves. We might, in other words, look freshly at both microscopic and macroscopic events without being too bound in our observations by what the teacher or the students believe is happening.

Changeableness. Another feature of the type of evaluative orientations under discussion is their changeableness. This is not to imply that they do not exhibit stability as well. Yet though human preferences and motivations do tend to remain relatively the same from one situation to the next, it is also true that they can and do undergo dramatic transformations from time to time. In this respect they differ very markedly from the more ordinary type of academic change that educators are accustomed to thinking about and planning for. Formal knowledge may be forgotten, abilities may fade with time, skills may decay through disuse, but these forms of gradual erosion do not begin to compare with the sudden shifts in interest and general outlook that the teacher might witness several times during a single school term. Moreover, whereas the growth of complex abilities and knowledge seems to pass through a series of definable stages moving from the simple to the more complex, with each increment helping to ensure the stability of the entire structure, there appears to be no comparable evolutionary model to depict the life cycle of these other forms of change.

This classic difference between states of knowing and states of appraising has profound implications for the important educational task of establishing goals and objectives. Indeed, the very concepts of goals and objectives, with their hint of spatial and temporal reality, may not be nearly as useful for thinking about evaluative orientations, such as attitudes and feelings, as they have proved to be when applied to the business of nurturing academic growth.

When teachers report that a student has reached an educational goal, such as the acquisition of a certain level of reading competence, most of the reactions appropriate to the attainment of a physical goal are quite in keeping and even expected. Although the occasion may not have the drama of conquering a mountain or winning a race, the newly successful reader is assumed to have expended a certain amount of energy in his effort and he is entitled (assuming he appreciates what he has done) to feel a sense of accomplishment. Friends and admirers, if they wish, may offer messages of congratulations and praise. Moreover, once the job is done it is done, and nothing but the ravages of memory loss and exotic internal disturbances, such as retroactive inhibition, can undo it.

Consider, however, the situation that holds when the "objective" in question is some modification of a student's appraisal of something. Suppose, for example, his teacher discovers that Johnny has developed an intense interest in reading books about knighthood, following a project on that topic in social studies. Let us even suppose that the teacher had desired this to happen and had done what he could to encourage such an interest. Is it fitting to think of this change as an accomplishment on the part of the student? Is a sense of pride appropriate? Are messages of congratulations and praise in order? I think not.

This does not mean that both the teacher and the student might not be pleased about what has taken place. The teacher might even communicate his pleasure to the student, thus adding an additional source of gratification to that derived from the new-found interest. But both parties behave very differently than they might on the occasion of the attainment of an academic goal. Also, quite often they both realize that the student's new interest is a temporary state of affairs. By next month, or certainly by next year, Johnny could well be fed up with the adventures of Sir Galahad and his contemporaries; instead, he may have discovered a new source of pleasure in tales of science fiction. The teacher usually expects such a change to take place and is not at all upset about it when it happens. Indeed, he may even encourage the student to abandon the very interest he labored so hard to cultivate a few months previously. In so doing he is behaving in a way that is quite unlike his practice with respect to the attainment of achievement goals.

These differences and others lead me to believe that all of our talk about goals and objectives is misdirected when applied to those secondary consequences involving the student's evaluative appraisal of himself and his world. This does not mean that I think teachers should stop talking about what they would like to see happen to their students. But I see no reason why they should be burdened with the precise definition of pedagogical end-states in a domain of human behavior where concepts such as level of proficiency, terminal behavior, and the like are quite inappropriate. The metaphoric use of concepts like goals and objectives may have its place in certain types of educational discussions, but it does little good to encourage people to chase rainbows simply because that has been shown to be an effective strategy for catching a bus.

Duration. The ephemeral quality of a rainbow is an appropriate image with which to introduce a third and final feature of the class of secondary consequences under consideration. For, like rainbows, many of these consequences are of very brief duration, often lasting barely long enough to be witnessed by the alert teacher. Here I have in mind particularly those fleeting shifts of mood and interest that seem to affect the extent of the students' attention to classroom activities and his involvement in the work at hand. These vagaries of feeling have to do with the student's evaluation of specific experiences—*this* lesson, *this* textbook, *this* assignment—rather than his more generalized dispositions toward whole classes of events. Thus, it is possible for a student to like math but not to feel like doing his arithmetic assignment, to dislike history but to get caught up, almost despite himself, in a classroom discussion of the origins of the Civil War. (These minor contradictions, incidentally, are often the occasion for feigned surprise on the part of teachers and parents, who are likely then to remark, "I thought you liked math," or "I thought you disliked history." The student is expected to respond with chagrin and to admit that maybe he does or does not like the subject after all.)

The relationship between these short-term and long-term phenomena is poorly understood and poses intriguing questions for the practitioner. How, for example, should he divide his attention between the two? If he concentrates on establishing and maintaining the student's immediate interests and involvement in the task at hand, will the long-term consequences take care of themselves? Or, conversely, if he insists that students work when they are disinterested or unwilling, is he inadvertently contributing to a consequence he will later deplore? Is not the teacher's outlook future-directed almost by definition and, therefore, does not a focus on the immediate quality of the student's experience contradict this essential aspect of his professional orientation, placing him in a role akin to that of the entertainer or babysitter?

Components of Education

This last question calls attention to two important components of school experience: the *preparatory* and the *consummatory*. The official purpose of education is doubtlessly preparatory. That is, the chief reason for spending all those thousands of hours in classrooms is to prepare us for the life we will lead outside them. Yet the very fact that the amount of time we spend there is measured in thousands of hours rather than in minutes or seconds means that we cannot brush aside questions concerning the quality of the experience itself. Moreover, these questions are logically quite independent of what that experience does to the enhancement of our future performance or to the enduring attitudes and values that stay with us long after the last dismissal bell has rung.

In other words, even if the immediate comfort or discomfort of students were totally unrelated to the long-term consequences of schooling, we might still want to concern ourselves with these consummatory aspects of classroom life simply because the act of going to school accounts for so large a portion of human existence. The tragedy implicit in some adults' recollections of their life in school has less to do with the marks left on them by the experience than with what schooling did or did not do to the quality of their childhood as they lived it. Thus, as we focus, with obvious justification, on the enduring consequences of schooling, let us not forget that the experience is itself enduring. For both students and teachers its consequences are here and now as well as in the future.

Here, then, are a few informal reflections on the question of what schooling does to people. I obviously do not know what influence, if any, these thoughts will have on the reader's way of thinking about this matter, but for myself the task of formulating them has had the effect of making me want to reexamine with greater care than I have done to date some of the popular assumptions and points of view that educators and others bring to their examination of how schools do and should operate. I am even more convinced than I was, for example, that many simplistic views of the educative process, commonly derived in a haphazard manner from the engineering sciences and often dressed up in the brassy lingo of the military strategist, are inadequate. They are not only inadequate as conceptual models but they are downright pernicious in the way they are used to discourage educational researchers and other competent people from tackling problems that cannot be easily phrased in terms of "inputs" and "outputs" and made quantifiable by the introduction of a couple of paper and pencil tests. The field of education, in my opinion, does not need better tests and more sophisticated research designs nearly as badly as it needs new ways of looking at some of its oldest problems. How to come to grips with the non-academic consequences of schooling is surely one of these.

Curriculum as Educational Process: The Middle Class Against Itself

EDGAR Z. FRIEDENBERG

TWO of the most relevant comments on the unstudied curriculum to have come to my attention were made by Marshall McLuhan with reference to perception and communication generally: his most familiar aphorism that "The medium is the message"; and another, only slightly less frequently quoted, "We don't know who discovered water; but we're pretty sure it wasn't the fish."

The schools, in America, are the most ubiquitous and in many ways the most egregious of the mass media; and they are the only medium to have a wholly captive audience and to be totally government controlled, though by local rather than national government. And as McLuhan's phrase implies, their message lies in the experience of attending them day after day, year after year, under coercion that makes it unlawful even to exist if you are under sixteen and happen to go anywhere else in order to do it. What the schools teach students deliberately—which is often either unintelligible or incredible on the basis of the students' earlier experience—is simply insignificant compared with what they teach by virtue of the massive fact of their existence, and the smugness with which they police what has now become the only permitted route to maturity. Every youngster in an industrialized state today is taught —and well taught—that he must travel through time like an American traveling along the one allowable access road across East Germany to West Berlin, monitored by guards at every checkpoint. A dropout is considered either as a breakdown or a criminal and, in either case, must be prevented from finding out whether he could make it on his own by bushwhacking. Yet, it is just a century since the Kalamazoo decision made it lawful even to spend public funds for secondary education, much less to require all persons to accept it.

What is most distinctive about the schools as compared to other social institutions is their totality. No other institution—for even the Selective Service System and the armed services limit their compulsion to males—presumes to require unremunerated attendance and observance of its rituals by an entire age group for more than a decade, under penalty of either criminal or economic sanctions. Even life out of school is in many ways effectively controlled by regulations, like those governing hair length, which have only the most devious connection if any with the school's manifest instructional purpose, but which permit its value systems and its peculiar folkways to invade all other spheres of the pupils' life. It is assumed that no experience that occurs out of school and without the explicit consent of its administration can have sufficient educational value to justify the pupil or his parents in allowing the pupil to cut school in order to take part in it. What the student learns is that the state has simply preempted the right to determine the pattern of his life, though it occasionally permits parents to negotiate an opportunity to make small, temporary, variations in it.

In 1969 in New York City, the school board unilaterally assumed the right to extend school hours and to cancel traditional holidays in order to permit teachers, and require students, to "make up" the time lost through the teachers' patently unlawful strike. The only thing that will be demonstrably regained by this is the payment the teachers forfeited by striking; the educational benefits are more uncertain. Family and pupil plans will be disrupted; and it is a safe conjecture that some of the time will be spent by teachers instructing their pupils in the sanctity of authority, the need for law and order, and the folly of permitting any dissident group to select which laws it will obey.

Functions of Schooling

While the unusually arbitrary action of the New York City School Board may be attributed to emergency, its meaning nevertheless cannot be dismissed by treating it as an isolated event. It is precisely in an emergency that we must make open, public choices among the values we wish to preserve; and what the Board chose to preserve was the hegemony and financial security of its bureaucracy, not the educational reforms introduced by the imaginative staffs and parents of the experimental districts. Moreover, the regime regularly imposed on students is in its own way as arbitrary as the new demands on parents; its rhythms are simply more familiar. Domination of the life-patterns of the young—and through them, to a lesser degree, of their elders—by the schools is unnoticed, not because it is infrequent, ineffectual, or rare, but because it performs a useful set of functions that society, in fact, depends on but which conflict with its ideology and hence with the self-image of many of its members—particularly with the self-images of school personnel themselves.

Socialization of the Young

The first of these functions is the definition of youth as youth and childhood as childhood; the establishment of persons below school-leaving age *in statu pupillari,* which is one of the lowest statuses in our society. When colored by other pejoratively defined social traits, as in the case of poor, black youth, it becomes *the* lowest; it becomes abject. Yet any individual under 21 in this country is subject to sanctions and controls, and is denied certain rights that are granted by law to every other citizen. Legally, the juvenile code, for example, provides for summary and arbitrary treatment of juveniles whose conduct is disapproved by school or police officials, and affords few, if any, of the procedural safeguards formally provided—though often unavailable—to adult accused.[1]

---

[1] While it is true that legal procedure for adults, as well as for juveniles, has been institutionalized in ways that make it more responsive to the needs of the court bureaucracies—including opposing counsel—than to the formal rights of the litigants (cf. Abraham S. Blumberg, "Covert Contingencies in the Right to the Assistance of Counsel," *Law and Society Review* 2: 15-39; 1967), the existence of these formal rights still markedly affects the course of legal process. The law governing juveniles, however, seems expressly designed to subject them to the control of the lowest echelons of officials in the institutions intended to control them, and to deny them any effective process by which they might contest the actions of those officials. The most complete account of this process known to me is Aaron V. Cicourel, *The Social Organization of Juvenile Justice* (New York: John Wiley & Sons, 1968). It must of course be granted, as Cicourel does, that quite comparable practices are common enough in dealing with poor adults suspected of crimes or merely found to be a serious nuisance; and that society relies on these informal means of keeping them in line to prevent its legal system from collapsing under the strain of processing their defenses, should they choose to assert their putative rights (cf. Jerome Skolnick, *Justice Without Trial.* New York: John Wiley & Sons, 1966).

CURRICULUM AS EDUCATIONAL PROCESS

Yet without the school, and compulsory school attendance, the juvenile code would be a much less effective constraint. Together, they establish a set of offenses that only a schoolchild can commit; they create a presumption of guilt if a youngster is found out of school during school hours—however innocent his conduct—and they make any effective protest by the young against the conditions that prevail in their school unlawful *per se*. That these disabilities reflect the prevailing will of adult society is self-evident; but it is less immediately obvious *why* this should be so.

Relatively brief reflection, however, reveals that the adult society derives several advantages from the definition of "youth" as a subject class. Indeed, many of these advantages are not only familiar but have been legitimated ideologically, so that they are assumed to be services to youth rather than constraints upon it. There is the obvious fact that the experience of schooling and its routines develops in the young and malleable the skills and the disposition to fill the social roles that exist in the status-system of the present society, while weakening by anxiety and attrition their power to conceive of alternative social arrangements. Positively, this is called socialization, which may well be defined as the systematic extinction of alternatives. The current emphasis on the failure of the educational system to meet the needs of the "disadvantaged" and the "culturally deprived" is long overdue in recognizing the immiserization of these young people by the hostility and contempt most schools display toward them and their state of sullen and rebellious captivity within the schools. Yet awareness of this failure has the adverse effect of blinding the schools even further to the moral ambiguity of their own intervention. The current literature on the education of the disadvantaged is more critical than before of the means of education, but less critical of the ends.

This literature urges technical improvement in the use of language and methods of instruction which members of the underclass will find more alluring so that they will experience at least the illusion of success and not drop out as readily. Such literature becomes more intolerant of questions about whether the school *should* in fact compel young people to become the kind of adults the society can use with least trouble in its factories and armies and the routine rituals of democracy. An idealistic or romantic critic of our schools is apparently one who is not prepared to concede that the schools ought to be empowered to compel the poor to take advantage of their opportunities to the end that they may become indistinguishable from Mr. Nixon's supporters—or school principals. In America, today, this may be the only pathway to equality of economic opportunity at lower levels; but it does not exhaust the possibilities of diverse human development—it merely usurps them.

Provision of Economic Opportunity

Still compulsory, total immersion in school routines for 13 years or more does, in the narrow sense, contribute to economic opportunity up to a point—though I shall later argue that its effect on the kinds of traits and character-structure needed for really "making it" may be more ambiguous. It contributes to the economic opportunity of the poor, for whom even lower-middle class life and status may be an improvement, if hardly a pleasure. And beyond any possible debate it contributes to the economic opportunity of the public school bureaucracy. We should all be very grateful, I think, to the New York City teachers and their union for making it clear how precious and really fundamental to their concerns their economic interests really are. There is, of course, nothing either specially new or specially crass about their response to threats to their position.

It is not, as Amitai Etzioni has shown,[2] unusual for a bureaucracy to become more concerned with meeting the needs of its incumbents than of its clients, and to take such steps as lie within its power to resist their demands. But where the client is involuntary and the organization morally pretentious, its pretensions are likely to be shattered along with the clients' few remaining illusions.

What remains is the unpleasant possibility that American educational policy is extremely resistant to change for precisely the same reason that our military policy is: at 30 billion dollars a year, it is simply too expensive, profitable, and well-entrenched to be substantially altered by the demands of a politically powerless clientele. Public embarrassment may indeed force it to relax its efforts in one sector while cautiously extending them in another; but our educators are not, I think, about to admit even as a tentative hypothesis that any significant proportion of persons under the age of 18 might simply need to be free of their ministrations in order to work out the terms of their own lives. In this sense students are

[2] Amitai Etzioni. *Modern Organizations*. Englewood Cliffs, New Jersey: Prentice-Hall, Inc., 1964. pp. 94-104.

not just, as in Jerry Farber's phrase, "niggers," but "gooks" as well: coolies who are expendable as long as the overall project in which they have been coercively enrolled can be justified, to the satisfaction of those who now control it, as conducive to their incorporation in the American way of life and their ultimate opportunity to share what—if it is to keep going economically at all—must be accepted as its benefits.

School as Instrument of the Middle Class

Thus the school, as the instrument which defines youth *in statu pupillari*, confers two related advantages on the adult society as a whole. It socializes youth to take its place in an egalitarian gerontocracy; and it sets up an enormous and ubiquitous industry—not as large as the armed forces but much more equitably distributed throughout the land. In so doing, it perpetuates the norms by which the present distribution of power is legitimated. But the way in which the school does this calls into question its own legitimacy, and into even graver question the cordial relationship which has so long prevailed between the school and the middle class.

The school system has come to be treated as *par excellence* the faithful instrument of middle-class socialization, by its critics, including myself, as well as its admirers. And so, on the whole, it has been. Yet, as one looks more closely at the relationship between the school and the middle class, their continued collaboration begins to seem paradoxical. Like Bernard Shaw's celebrated liaison with Mrs. Patrick Campbell, it seems a convenience rather than a source of satisfaction; and I am not sure that it can continue to be either in sufficient degree to command the level of middle-class support needed for continued expansion.

Paradox of Collaboration

Relatively speaking the schools are getting dowdier; and they show no corresponding reluctance to impose their dowdiness on others. Even though public expenditures for education have increased fivefold since 1950, while enrollments have barely doubled, the schools have by and large clung to the folkways of the least affluent of the respectable classes, rejecting with mixed abhorrence and condescension the life styles of the "disadvantaged" and the "privileged" alike. Yet during this time a relatively privileged life style, or at least a simulacrum of it, has come to prevail among the upper ranges of the middle class and especially among its youth. The mass media have validated that style; the phenomenal growth of folk-rock as both an art form and a *lingua franca* that the middle-aged have been too contemptuous to learn has provided the young with a valuable windfall of unaccustomed privacy in communicating among themselves; meanwhile, the school's consistent and abominable record of what, in dealing with adults, would be unconscionable violations of civil liberty has impaired its authority among the relatively libertarian upper-middle classes.

All this is done, to be sure, in the name of preparing young people for the demands of adult life. "School," guidance counselors affirm, "is a business; and we must learn to behave in school in a businesslike way, and to dress and speak as an employer would expect." The most obvious implication of this rather common position is surely that compulsory school attendance conflicts with laws forbidding child labor. But in any case, it is clear that the kind of life-in-business that the schools envisage as they train the young to fit into it is not the life of a technician like a computer programmer, for example, whose skills guarantee him a degree of personal freedom, much less that of a professional or even an executive. It is the life of a clerk in the lower levels of bureaucracy or of a rather pinched small businessman.

Part of the recent enthusiasm of educational leaders for new programs for getting at the "disadvantaged" and "culturally deprived" arises, I am sure, from the fact that, since these are "deprived" by definition, it seems hardly necessary to justify the school's right and obligation to remake them into a more serviceable commodity; which will, indeed, improve their prospects of employment within the existing social system and diminish their urge to seek revolutionary changes in it. Yet it is rather less clear that this training improves the life-chances of middle-class youth even economically, and increasingly clear that it impairs them emotionally and aesthetically. For middle-class young people, school is the worst remaining hang-up and drag. While corporate employers buy advertising space to assure prospective employees that they don't have to wear grey flannel suits and short hair to get a job, and hold conferences to try to work out ways of improving their image among college seniors so that the current decline in interest in business careers may be halted, schools go on hassling students about what, for their age group, are quite conventional and expressive styles of dress and behavior—in the name of preparing them to meet the demands of employment. In fact, the potential leadership of the country depends on those youngsters who possess the wit and style to defend their private lives against intrusive authorities, of which the school is only the first, though often the most presumptuous, of many.

A Lower-Middle Class Place

There is, of course, much more at issue here than taste. The function of school routines is to link the student's self-esteem to his ability to accept lower-middle class values and styles of life without rebelling against them or becoming a troublemaker; and the success with which the school achieves this mission is attested by the student's credentials. I do not mean by this that working-class students get the best grades and letters of recommendation. They don't, though teachers often prefer to have them in class because they tend to be neater and more docile. The best credentials go to relatively higher status students who are willing to adjust to common-man routines without making trouble, and who are content to skim off the cream of privilege without embarrassing the cows or complaining about how the dairy is run or becoming curious about how it fits into the economy as a whole.

To raise embarrassing or controversial questions is enough, of itself, to betray a failure in socialization. For this reason most school administrators find it very difficult, I am convinced, to understand that a civil liberties issue might arise in their school. They could not recognize one if they saw it, since the students' insistence that they, too, had a right to dress according to their taste or to invite the assembly speaker they wanted to hear or to print and distribute their own uncensored newspaper is defined as either misconduct or bad judgment, which it is the school's responsibility to help them by correcting. Basically, schools are lower-middle class places; and civil liberty is not a lower-middle class thing.

School administrators do not take seriously student—or even parental—claims that they are entitled to certain freedoms of personal expression; they dismiss such claims as one more effort by a privileged class to harass them into tolerating behavior that the community would not put up with. Generally they are right about what community standards are, in this too-often sour, shabby, envy- and anxiety-ridden society. But the middle class, though as envious and anxiety-ridden as any, is getting a little less sour and a lot less shabby; moreover, it is really worried about the generation gap. And the schools, with their petty regulations, and locker searches, and eager cooperation with police and undercover narcotics agents, with their hospitality to military recruiters and hostility to student protest against the war or the draft, are making the generation gap worse by turning the brighter and more critical-minded and socially responsive kids off like a faucet. The boy who has been suspended from school for wearing a protest button or an armband loses his opportunity to hear the Marine recruiter, in dress uniform and medals, tell the assembled school what a wonderful job we are doing in Southeast Asia in spite of harassment from pukes like him. This adds, no doubt, to his respect for law and order; but it also helps make it clear to him, and perhaps even to his parents, that this year he is not getting much for his share of the 30 billion dollars.

A Middle-Class Dilemma

The puzzling question, for me, is why the middle class continues to put up with modes of socialization in school that prepare its youngsters for the style of life it is trying to escape and subjugates them to persons whose values, language, and patterns of anxiety identify them as status-inferiors. It is difficult, to be sure, for it to do anything else. Middle-class conservatives doubtless want this to happen, since they like to see their children kept in line; while middle-class liberals would feel too guilty about putting the schools down on a matter of class privilege. In America, however, freedom *is* an upper-middle class taste; the working class prefers Mayor Daley or George Wallace; and to claim freedom is to claim a privilege. I suspect that one of the major reasons for the flight of the middle classes to the suburbs is to do something about this dilemma without having to confront it directly.

The American middle class is notably finky and indecisive in facing any moral conflict; and so far as its members are governed by any ideology, that ideology is liberal and meliorist, and requires both that they remain in the city in order to preserve it from ruin and that they send their children to its schools to learn not to think they are any better than anybody else. But social classes, here as elsewhere, have their own special interests and seldom manage to remain unaware of them or to behave wholly counter to them. Tocqueville noted:

The Americans hold that in every state, the supreme power ought to emanate from the people; but when once that power is constituted, they can conceive, as it were, no limits to it, and they are ready to admit that it has the right to do whatever it pleases. They have not the slightest notion of peculiar privileges granted to cities, families, or persons: their minds appear never to have foreseen that it might be possible not to apply with strict uniformity the same laws to every part of the state, and to all its inhabitants.

But the flight to the suburbs seems to me intelligible as an oblique effort to set some limits to the crushing demands of an egalitarian society by interposing a limited local sovereignty of a slightly more generous order; and to create a town which, compared to the city, may afford its families, for a time, the peculiar privilege of a less brutal police and a less uptight school system than the city supports. What seems to me wrong with this solution is not that it is undemocratic but that it is neurotic—it evades the demands of the democratic superego instead of working them through until its tyranny is revealed.

Until suburban families accept the fact that they have indeed fled from a populace whose way of life and social institutions were strangling them, they cannot really become sufficiently aware of what they are doing to build institutions of their own that are much better. In a few years, the suburban school bureaucracy which shares, after all, the values and attitudes of the pedagogical community will have managed to make the suburban schools like those of the city even while the district it serves retains its suburban character.

The School as Source of Alienation

Yet the middle class has no conceivable need for such schools. Neither, perhaps, does anybody else whose children attend them. I have indicated that I believe the schools to be more useful to their own bureaucracies, and in providing society with a cohesive pattern of anxieties and a docile working force, than they are to their students. Yet it is the middle-class, suburban students who have become consciously aware that the school is a serious drag; so, to be sure, have many of the underclass—especially the blacks—but they seem less ready to write off its economic promise. They need the skills it has traditionally provided the ambitious poor; and the school may yet come to terms with them and learn to teach them, if only to preserve its *raison d'être*. But those terms will not be generous unless citizens learn to use the political instrumentality of the suburban school district to force from the schools a new model of respect for students—and of greater respect than common American practice accords youth.

Black people will, I hope, simultaneously and effectively continue their demands for humanization of the urban schools, while those black families who have already come to prefer the established middle-class pattern should, of course, be given every facility should they wish to move to the suburbs. But they are unlikely at this point to be able to buck the school system as effectively as those middle-class students who have come to perceive it as a prison rather than a gateway to opportunity; or their parents who have come to perceive the school system as the source of much of their alienation from their children. It has always been that, for its historic function is the Americanization of the sons and daughters of immigrants. But in performing that function, it represented the triumph of the new over the old, and this had at least the wistful assent of the older generation which had come seeking a new world.

Today, the schools alienate many young people—and especially middle-class young people—from the generation of their parents for precisely the opposite reason—by embodying a set of coercive demands that they perceive as exploitative, stupid, and, above all, obsolete and irrelevant to their lives. And some parents, I believe, are coming to realize that this is not only a rather strange service to purchase from the state at so high a price, but a rather perverse relationship to force on people who are not, whatever else they may be, consenting adults.

The Impact of School Philosophy and Practice on Child Development[1]

BARBARA BIBER
PATRICIA MINUCHIN

WE PLAN to discuss here the main points of a research study that assessed the impact of different styles of education on the psychological development of children. The history of this study goes back into the earlier years of the century when new and sometimes dramatic ideas were being introduced into the educational field. Influenced by new social forces and new psychological insights, some educators began to revise their vision of the educational process. They began to see the function and organization of school in different terms, reflecting their new understanding of child development, the nature of motivation and learning, and the complexity of personality formation.

Such ideas, and the methods that followed from them, registered unevenly on the various schools of the nation. These ideas and methods were unnoticed or rejected by many but absorbed or modified and carried forth by others. The net result is that, at any given moment of time, children of the same age going to school in America may be having very different school experiences—and this is true even within the group of white, middle-class children going to school in the same city. Though their schools may share certain broad features, they may at the same time differ basically

---

[1] The study presented in this paper was supported by the National Institute of Mental Health (grant #M1075), and is reported fully in a recently published book entitled *The Psychological Impact of School Experience* by P. Minuchin, B. Biber, E. Shapiro, and H. Zimiles, New York: Basic Books, 1969. Some sections of this paper are taken directly from the book.

27

in very important ways—in the ways they define education, the goals they have for the children, the methods they use to teach them, the relationships they maintain, the way they organize the school day, the total atmosphere they set up for teaching and learning. Some of these differences are explicit; others are implicit, often unidentified, generally unstudied.

It was these pervasive differences in school philosophy and practice that interested us and provided the impetus for the study. The research was set up to analyze differences in school environment, and to assess the impact of different kinds of schools on the children who attended them.

In this paper we will describe the school environments and present a portion of the findings about the children. First, however, it is necessary to state the nature of the study design, provide a framework for the substantive material to follow, and define the principal concepts of the study.

The Design of the Study

In designing the study, we decided to conduct an intensive study in a limited number of settings; this would allow us to look at the environment and the children in some detail and to explore many facets of their functioning. We therefore selected four schools that represented variations in educational philosophy and method. We conceived of these differences as occurring principally along a continuum of modern-traditional ideology and practice. This continuum constituted the independent variable of the study and is defined in detail as follows:

THE MODERN-TRADITIONAL ORIENTATION: DEFINITIONS

The *traditional* orientation has been conceived as centering on the socialization of the child, through known and standardized methods, toward generally approved forms of behavior and established levels of achievement. By this orientation, adults carry their authority role as one with fixed and unquestionable prerogatives for decisions of right and wrong and for the induction of the young into the established adult world. Child behavior is evaluated in terms of its external impact and its conformity to general standards, and individual differences are seen largely in terms of distance from or correspondence with these preconceived standards and levels of expectation.

The school, in this traditional framework, defines its task in the realm of intellectual growth. It conceives of an established body of knowledge as constituting the intellectual content of the culture and defines intellectual growth in terms of mastery of this subject matter.

It assumes a relatively direct training to be the pathway to such mastery. It evaluates pupil progress in comparative and competitive terms, and it tends to foster competition among the children for the approval and recognition of achievement, regarding other aspects of peer interaction as distractions from concentration and learning. It sees the teacher as the fixed authority in whom reside both the content of learning and the judgment of progress.

The *modern* orientation draws its philosophy from relatively contemporary understanding of the complex and dynamic forces involved in human behavior, learning, and growth. It expects a more complicated, uneven, and personally determined growth process and it sets a different balance between the general requirements of socialization and the needs and tendencies of the individual child. It incorporates the general view that the child will make his own life, that he will grow into a world different from the one he was born into, and that he must be capable both of adapting to it in a personally meaningful way and of making his impact upon it.

In keeping with this orientation, adults attempt to carry their authority role in a relatively flexible way; they relate more intimately with children, tolerate more challenge, and though they do not conceive of themselves as abdicating their role or functioning as peers, they are more consciously geared to ceding authority gradually as it becomes appropriate, manageable, and constructive for growth. This philosophy evaluates child behavior in terms of its motivation and meaning, as well as its social impact, and sees the individual child primarily in terms of his own pattern of interests, needs, capacities, and rate of growth.

The goals of a school, in this modern framework, are relatively broad. They involve the intellectual growth of the child, the education of his capacity to live and work with others, and the fostering of his development as a confident learner, as a person of unique skills and interests, and as a mature human being. The modern school stresses intellectual exploration and a probing toward integrative principles and depth of knowledge as much as it stresses the mastery of subject matter. It tends to explore new methods, to base its curriculum on understanding of the dynamics of child development, and to offer a variety of pathways and media for the achievement of mastery. It evaluates pupil progress primarily against a profile of the individual's strengths and weaknesses and only secondarily against group norms. It regards the peer group as a vital force for growth and learning, to be nurtured as such, and sees the teacher-child relationship as pivotal in the learning process and as best enacted in a way that is informed, flexible, and relatively close to the children.

The study was conducted in a large city; three of the schools were chosen from the public school system. The choice of a modern private school as the fourth school raised some research problems, but it seemed imperative to include a school that would have had time and opportunity to develop a stable and clear version of modern education. The obvious candidates for this most modern end of the continuum lay within the group of private schools, which inevitably have greater leeway to pursue and consolidate new ideas.

We made two other important decisions early in the planning of the study. The first concerned the socioeconomic background of the children. Since the children of the modern private school came from middle-class and upper-middle-class families, it was essential to choose children for the rest of the study who came from similar homes. We therefore chose public schools for the study from among those that served predominantly middle-class populations.

The other important decision concerned the age level of the children to be studied. We wanted to study children who had been in school long enough to reflect the cumulative effects of their school experience but who would not present the psychological complications of adolescence. For this reason we chose fourth-grade children—nine to ten years old. As the accompanying chart indicates, there were 105 study children—57 boys and 48 girls, distributed in the four schools. The schools are identified by fictitious names and brief descriptions of their positions on the modern-traditional continuum (see Chart 1).

Schools	Subjects of Study		
	Boys	Girls	Total
CONRAD—a small independent school which had, for many years, exemplified *modern* educational values	17	12	29
DICKENS—a large public school, outstanding in adapting *modern* concepts and methods within the practical limitations of its operation	12	12	24
ADAMS—a large public school which had added a few elements of the modern approach to its fundamentally *traditional* concepts and practices	18	16	34
BROWNING—a small public school which, relatively unaffected by modern trends, valued and sustained *traditional* methods	10	8	18
	57	48	105

Chart 1. The Study Schools and Subjects

Research material was collected in four areas through the efforts of four research teams. One team studied the schools as

THE IMPACT OF SCHOOL PHILOSOPHY AND PRACTICE 31

social institutions, gathering material through observations and interviews. On the basis of selection criteria the schools had been assigned relative positions on the modern-traditional continuum. But we continued to study them over a two-year period, while the rest of the research was being conducted, as a way of understanding more fully what the school environment was like for the children.

A second team observed throughout the academic year in the fourth-grade classrooms from which we drew our subjects. They took records in a variety of academic and nonacademic situations, recording the events and processes of the classroom and the activities of the study children.

A third team gathered material from the parents of the study children. They administered a questionnaire and interviewed each mother, in a session of about an hour and a half that covered her views about her child and her child-rearing attitudes and practices. This material was meant to give us some understanding of the relative impact of home and school on the areas of psychological functioning we were investigating, or at least to provide data on areas where home and school influence appeared to interact.

The fourth area of data collection concerned the children and was the crucial one. The main test of school impact, after all, lay in the internalized effects on the children—the attitudes and reactions that were becoming part of them as functioning personalities. We attempted to tap this kind of impact through a series of sessions with each child. The research team saw each child six times, interviewing him about his life and ideas and opinions, and administering a series of tests. These included tests of intelligence and achievement; a series of problem-solving tasks; projective techniques such as drawings and imaginative stories and a play session; and a variety of other psychological techniques that tapped the child's moral judgments, his aesthetic preferences, his attitudes about school and authority, and his image of himself and his own development. This, in broad terms, was the design and scope of the study. It might be important to mention two more points.

We had a set of expectations about the impact of different educational experiences, and we made a series of predictions about how children of modern and traditional schools might differ from each other in their functioning and development. We based these predictions on both explicit and implicit features of modern and traditional schools. Some examples of these predictions and their rationale will appear in connection with discussion of the findings.

Second, the study was planned as a systematic assessment of

school effects and incorporated as much scientific rigor as the problem would allow. A study conducted in naturalistic field situations faces certain obvious limitations in the control it can exert over conditions; furthermore, when it has multiple and complex purposes, such as assessing personality development, it faces some uncertainty in measurement. Nonetheless, data were gathered and handled with all possible precautions. For instance, all records on the children were masked before analysis, so that we did not know the identity of the child, his school, or his sex. In addition, all findings were subjected to statistical tests. The material was analyzed through analysis of variance, assessing the significance of differences between the school groups and between the sexes. Measures on the children were correlated with measures of parental attitude, to provide a framework for evaluating the relative impact of the school. In this presentation the findings will be summarized without reference to statistics or significance levels. These statements, however, are based on the systematic analysis of the research material and the statistical establishment of differences among children from the different schools.

The School Environments

On the basis of the design we had set ourselves we faced two central questions: What kind of school description is relevant to our proposition concerning the school's comprehensive impact as a life environment? How is a concept such as modern-traditional ideology expressed in concrete teaching-learning events?

The distinctions between modern and traditional ideology as applied to school functioning, drawn up in general terms in the initial phase of the study, were adequate as criteria for selecting the study schools. The principals of 24 candidate schools were interviewed. The facts gathered were, on the face of it, common garden variety information about school functioning: admissions procedures, curriculum overview, how supervision is carried out, most desired qualifications in teachers, most needed new facilities, the school's primary goals for the children. Yet, among 24 schools, 20 of them under a common board of education, wide contrasts in basic orientation came through clearly. The schools differed widely in the vision of what constitutes intellectual competence and how children can be motivated to learn, with respect to how authority relations are mediated and how the balance is weighted between supporting individuality and emphasizing socialization.

THE IMPACT OF SCHOOL PHILOSOPHY AND PRACTICE 33

By design, all four schools shared certain common characteristics: comparable parent populations, relatively stable administrations, and reputations as good schools. They were characterized as having reasonably benign attitudes toward children, and the task of teaching was perceived as a serious professional responsibility. The schools were different in size and neighborhood setting, but these differences did not correspond to their positions on educational ideology. For example, one of the two *small* schools was the most modern, the other *small* school was most traditional.

The criteria for selecting the schools had been preliminary and fairly general. It remained for the study of the schools to identify the dimensions of school experience considered most relevant to our thesis of broad psychological impact, to translate these dimensions into terms of school functioning, and to describe their condition in each of the four study schools.

The collection of the data and their subsequent analysis were governed by a schema consisting of a series of functional categories which defined school practices and values, distinguishing modern from traditional emphases. Conceptually, the operational categories were dealt with as part of four major themes of school ideology. The following material deals with the three most important themes.

The first theme, "Education for Competence," represents our interest in how a school interprets its role: its viewpoint about achievement and mastery, its concern for motivation, its interest in creative processes, and its investment in variety of modes of learning.

The second theme, "Quality and Patterns of Interaction Among People," considers the mediation of authority between superiors and subordinates and the school's ways of engaging the children in their relations to each other: the relative flexibility of rules and regulations, the quality and purposes of discipline, the personalization of relationships, and the concern for peer group processes.

The third theme, "View of Individuality," considers the school's perspective on individual growth and development: the balance it sustains between socialization and strengthening of individual identity, its emphasis on the expression of individual interests, ideas, and feelings, its perception of personality and intellectual style, and its criteria for individual progress.

Chart 2 presents these three themes and offers selected examples of the guidelines for rating the schools. In each instance, the first stem of the example represents an illustration of the modern emphasis and the second stem the traditional.

Education for Competence

Stimulation of Intellectual Processes
(e.g., active exploration and discovery by the child *vs.* direct transmission of information and skill from teacher to child)

Variety of Learning Modes
(e.g., variety of media for expressive activities *vs.* reliance on the verbal mode as the proper instrument for learning)

Sources of Motivation: Children
(e.g., stimulation of interest and self-investment in learning activity *vs.* use of established symbols as measure of accomplishment)

Sources of Motivation: Teachers
(e.g., sense of competence derived from depth and vigor of children's response to learning activities *vs.* pride in high achievement measures attained by children)

Encouragement of Teacher Autonomy
(e.g., teachers encouraged and supported in innovative, creative approaches to curriculum *vs.* teachers expected to follow a directed course in implementing objectives as interpreted by the administration).

Quality and Patterns of Interaction Among People

Authority in the Teacher-Child Relationship
(e.g., rules and regulations adapted functionally to meet needs of varied classroom activities *vs.* rules and regulations fixed to protect high standards of quiet and orderliness necessary to teacher-directed learning;

(e.g., use of disciplinary measures as corrective expedients intended to remedy disruption *vs.* punishment conceived as retribution for wrong done, presumed valuable for learning distinctions between right and wrong)

Authority in Administrator-Teacher Relationship
(e.g., emphasis on individualized working relationship for mediating authority *vs.* assumption that authority is based on the powers and responsibilities assigned to the office by a higher authority)

Use of Peer Groups in Organization of Children's Work
(e.g., engaging the class in problem solving and opinion formation involving codes of social behavior as well as study content *vs.* whole class organized as a formal unit engaged in individual question-answer exchange with teacher).

View of Individuality

Self-Realization and Socialization
(e.g., guiding and facilitating individual potential considered essential in teaching *vs.* adaptation to and compliance with preestablished codes considered the most important factor in socialization)

Perception of Children
(e.g., individualized descriptions in terms of qualities of personality, behavioral style, and intellectual characterization *vs.* children described in terms of brightness, IQ, social background, and behavior)

Theory Concerning Child Development and Deviation
(e.g., concepts of child development used as foundation for curriculum design and teacher role *vs.* early years seen as socializing preparation for intellectual mastery of later years).

Chart 2. Categories for Analysis of School Practices and Values

THE IMPACT OF SCHOOL PHILOSOPHY AND PRACTICE 35

The schools were compared and given consensus rankings on each category in the series. As the outcome of this analysis, the relative order assigned to the schools at the time they had been selected was corroborated, though the separation into two pairs was sharper than anticipated. Of the four schools selected to represent distinct positions in modern-traditional orientation, two appeared to occupy clearly polarized positions, two others represented modifications. While distinct as two pairs educationally, the members of each pair were of course not identical and the nature of the differences between the members of each pair was important in connection with interpretation of the findings on the children.

The outstanding characteristics of the two modern schools can be contrasted to the two traditional schools in the way their educational ideology was carried out. It is also possible to indicate briefly the way in which personality and value systems contributed to making each school a distinct environment for learning and a model for living.

Modern Schools: Physical Image

In our mind's eye there are clear physical images of the four schools. When we think of Conrad, referring to the most modern school, we see a group of renovated small family dwellings on a quiet side street, quite centrally located in a big city in a neighborhood with several mixes—ethnic, economic, and cultural. Small, as schools go, architecturally makeshift and improvised, this school nevertheless provided facilities for outdoor activities in the backyards, joined together behind the houses, and for special rooms set aside for music, shopwork, ceramics, and science in addition to graded classrooms.

Within this unconventional housing there was an atmosphere of high spirits—artwork of the children displayed on the walls; children moving about, talking, and laughing; sounds of recorder music mingled with noises that go with baseball.

When we think of Dickens, referring to the modern public school, we see a large old school building of an earlier era in poor physical shape, under fairly continuous condition of breakdown and repair, located adjacent to a middle-income housing development. Much had to be improvised in this setting to meet the educational needs of over 1500 children, but a quality of high vigor and amiability came through—in the tone of busy aliveness in the way the children and the adults moved about in the halls and, as at

Conrad, in the strong, emphatic color and design of the prolific artwork that was hung on the walls, overcoming the institutional drabness of the setting.

Traditional Schools: Physical Image

Turning to the traditional schools, Adams, another very large public school with quite a different image, presents itself: a new building, freshly painted in pastels with yellow-tiled hallways. In wide halls, glass-enclosed cases were placed at regular intervals in which children's products appeared with professionally prepared exhibits. Doors opened on well-equipped, light, airy rooms. Typical of urban patterns, the school was located in an immediate neighborhood of residential wealth which bordered, quite close by, on poor tenement dwellings. The school took its tone and most of its children from the upper-middle class segments—restrained, decorous, well-mannered, and well-cared-for.

Browning, the fourth and most traditional of the study schools, was located at a greater distance from the heart of the city, part of the small house-and-garden type of life that characterizes the outer regions of a large city. Like Conrad, it was small but bore little other resemblance to it. The building was in good condition, spacious, neat and clean—not new and architecturally sprightly like Adams nor deteriorated and drooping like Dickens. A quality of neutrality characterized building and atmosphere. The quiet halls were unembellished; children's work was not in evidence. It added up to a nondescript, almost barren institutional quality.

Traditional Schools: Educational Program

The traditional orientation to education was common to both Adams and Browning. In both schools, the measure of intellectual excellence was in the performance. Teaching was directed to a body of knowledge, as organized in textbooks and curriculum syllabi, to be mastered at a level that would make it available to recall and replication in its original form and meanings.

The teacher was the central figure—directing, organizing to the level of detail; the children's position was that of carrying out the specific learning tasks he established for them according to the given forms and standards that were defined as superior performance. Teaching was invested in developing proficiency in the basic operations of the word and number symbol systems, both regarded as essential prerequisites for the later more complex cognitive engagement with ideas in upper grades. These learning activities occupied most of the school hours, with children seated at desks or working at the blackboard. They constituted the primary sphere in which success or failure was experienced by the children and in which brightness or mediocrity was attributed to the children by the teachers. Several forces were expected to keep the children motivated to learn: wish for teacher approval, high grades symbolizing personal success and competitive strength, and secondary privileges granted to high-ranking children.

The two schools shared a common approach to methods of teaching and evaluation, with emphasis on accuracy and finish of performance and stimulation of competitive striving. They had similar goal priorities: to keep academic standing high in comparison to other schools and to be in control of behavior at all times in the school day.

In both, the teacher was a figure of authority, usually maintaining personal and status distance from the children, functioning within a clear system of right and wrong behavior. The values which had priority in this educational ideology were reflected in the way the children were perceived and characterized. Their individuality was defined in terms of relative brightness, academic prowess, and behavioral adaptability.

Beyond this common base, there were certain curriculum differences between the schools. Browning appeared, on the whole, untouched in its traditionalism, almost a pure form. There was minimal variety in the program—almost no activities that would be classified as creative and very little occasion to leave the classroom in which a sober, conscientious, quiet, orderly climate was consistently maintained for passively learning children.

At Adams, rated less traditional than Browning in several categories, there was a more complicated picture associated with its efforts to exemplify the best in public education. The program was more varied—there was a program of creative activities and an enthusiastic use of audio-visual materials with which the school was lavishly equipped. The children had more opportunity to be active, to find outlets for individual interests, but these activities were regarded as supplementary—a sort of cultural adjunct—not integral to the basic processes and purposes of education. The values attached to these activities had to do with the relative perfection of virtuosity, not expression of personal meaning.

These two schools were basically traditional, but they were

different in the nature of the life-style and ethos of the school as a social institution and life environment. At Browning, the teachers were the kind of people who naturally created an atmosphere of quiet plainness, conscientious application to assigned tasks, controlled feeling, and satisfaction with good performance on goals of limited scope. As a school, Browning appeared self-satisfied, unburdened by the tensions associated with striving for public recognition. The staff maintained a still-water atmosphere by insulating itself from the stimulating influences of the changing world of education.

At Adams, personal magnetism was included as one of the desirable teacher attributes. As professionals, the teachers were involved in conflicts of role; they meant to maintain distance as clear authority figures but at times engaged in personal exchanges with the children. They were most unified in their strong sense of audience, in wanting to keep their school a showplace in the public school system, and in their willingness to work for striking display in production and presentation. Obviously, children attending these two schools were exposed to very different modes and values of adult living.

Modern Schools: Educational Program

Turning back to the modern schools, Conrad was clearer and more consistent in its modern ways, closer to a theoretical model of a modern school than Dickens. At Conrad there had been many years of trying out new designs in curriculum, in classroom organization, and in teacher-child relationships as the appropriate means for accomplishing special educational goals. The changes they had introduced were built on their preference for those instructional methods—exploration, discovery, discussion—that aim to make learning an active process, challenging the child to independent search, experimentation, and complex cognitive maneuver between the beginning and end of intellectual tasks. These goals are easily recognized as forerunners of major contemporary trends.

The program was diversified; creative arts were a built-in feature of school life, fostered and valued as important modes of expression in the sense that they deepen sensitivity and integrate experience. Emphasis in the curriculum on active exploration, independent discovery, and personal expression was part of the tenet that an educational climate should match the basic modes and impulses of childhood.

The importance of the children to each other and as a "body politic," young as they were, was honored in the use of open group discussion to think through problems and share opinions, to plan for division of labor, to consider the injustice of a rule and find a reasonable revision. There was the opportunity to work intimately in small groups on tasks requiring cooperative attack, to fulfill collective responsibility.

In all, such practices made of these classrooms busy, active places, full of things in process of being made, ideas in process of being formed, and skills being mastered, with a teacher-leader and participant children keeping as much calm as was necessary for learning and work to be unhampered—what has been described as a workshop atmosphere.

The teachers tried to establish their authority role on a mutually acceptable working relationship between themselves as adults in charge and their pupils as growing children. They favored flexible rules and regulations, adaptable to different kinds of learning situations and not so restrictive as to appear unreasonable to the children. The strength of their authority depended not on punitive superiority nor the power of an impersonal system but rather on the building of an important relation between teacher and child—through the teacher's awareness of them as distinct personalities, through his willingness to be known to them as a person, and through his willingness to work through with them the problems inherent in the conflict between impulse and social requirements.

Dickens, operating as a large public school, was also ranked as a modern school, though consistently less modern than Conrad. The differences lay, not in goals or aspirations, but in the extent to which staff members were in a position to match their practices with their goals. The school was moving vigorously to adopt the techniques, relatively new to them, that bring the child as a learner to the foreground in the learning-teaching configuration, that accent opportunity for self-direction, and that vary the modes of learning experience. Dickens shared Conrad's conviction that learning tasks could be so interesting and stimulating that children would become deeply involved and motivated to learn for the sake of intrinsic pleasure and fulfillment, but teachers were not free to dispense with report cards.

Dickens was a large school, under mandate of regulations from a central board and going through a period of transition in which diverse viewpoints within the teaching faculty pulled in different directions. The modern trend, spearheaded and supported by an adventurous principal, was enacted through an enclave of teachers committed to modern views and practices, coexisting with other teachers who held traditional views and practices—almost a school within a school.

Yet, within this enclave of teachers, despite the uncertainty of transition and new beginnings, there were qualities of style and perspective and a hierarchy of values that were close to those of the Conrad teachers. These teachers expressed and enjoyed individual teaching style. They had come into teaching as a chosen profession in which they expected to invest their energies and from which they expected to derive personal gratification, and they saw themselves as part of a forward movement of change in education. They had a special bond in their sense of difference from the majority of their public school colleagues—a sense of difference that was based in their wish to vitalize the learning experience and bring the individual child into the foreground of the process.

Unique Features

The basic distinction between modern and traditional educational practices and values that characterized the two pairs of schools did not obscure the individual character and internal consistency of each one as a total environment. The greatest internal consistency appeared, as might be expected, at the extremes. Conrad's goal of educating autonomous, committed individuals who would retain the initiative to reshape social processes was consistently expressed in both the personal styles of the teachers and the school's credo for education. Browning's goal of carrying out its responsibility of educating skilled people who would accept and fit into the established social scheme was consistently honored in its idea systems and in the climate of human relations. In the other schools, Dickens and Adams, there was less internal coherence, less consistency in the way the children were being taught and the values people were living by.

The interaction between these forces is a dynamic one. The professional self-image, modes of work, and personalities of the people who man a school shape and color educational ideas and ideals.

In the last analysis, however, ideas and ideals are forceful shapers of institutions and eventually become the template to which people must fit.

Impact on the Children: Selected Study Findings

We come now to the question of impact on the children. What difference does it make in the life of a child to attend a modern or traditional school? What kinds of differences did we expect? What questions did we ask about the impact of the schools on the psychological growth of the children in our study?

The questions we asked and the predictions we made covered a broad range. We expected an impact on many facets of intellectual functioning, for example, on intellectual attitudes and styles of thinking; and we predicted that the impact of school experience would extend further to the formation of attitudes that the children would hold about other people, about themselves, their society, and their developing roles. We started with the obvious knowledge that the family and early experiences shape the child's personality and expectations profoundly by the time he enters school; and we attempted, as we looked at the data, to keep cognizance of this continuing family influence. But we considered that the child's experiences in school occupy much of his life-space during these years, and that from these complex and multileveled experiences he learns much and is partly formed as a person.

For purposes of this presentation we have chosen to concentrate on two aspects of the child data: the children's attitudes toward authority, control, and justice; and several aspects of self-image or identity. These have seemed particularly pertinent to a conference on the unstudied curriculum, since the differences we found probably stemmed in part from those aspects of life and relationship in school that have often been unspecified and unstudied but which probably have considerable impact on the growth and orientation of children.

Children's Attitudes

First, let us consider the findings concerning the children's conceptions of school authority and their developing codes of judgment concerning right and wrong, control, and justice. We drew our material in this area from interview, from a sentence completion test, and from simulated dilemma situations. The relevant items are presented in Chart 3.

In evaluating the children's attitudes toward rules and the authority structure of the school, we considered their responses to the Sentence Completion Test, categorizing them as: rebellious,

Children's Attitudes Toward School Authority
    Sentence Completion Test
        (a standard psychological technique, presenting incomplete sentences for the child to finish)
        Relevant Items:
            "When the teacher leaves the room . . ."
            "The day Betty (Ben) was late to school . . ."
            "Waiting in the principal's office, Emily (Ed) . . ."
            "When visitors came to Mary's (Jim's) class . . ."
            "Whenever the teacher asked for quiet . . ."

Codes of Control and Principles of Right and Wrong
    Sentence Completion Item: "I try not to . . ."
    Interview Question: "What's the very worst thing a child in your class could do?"
    Interview Question: "Can you think of something that you would call unfair?"
    Dilemma Situation: The children were asked to judge which of two children who were taking an important test did more wrong: the one who was seen by the teacher while looking at someone else's paper or the one who did the same thing but was not seen.

Chart 3. Methods and Material for Study of Children: Attitudes Toward School Authority, Codes of Control, and Principles of Right and Wrong [2]

resentful, conforming, or rational. We found clear differences among the school groups—or at least between the children of Conrad (the most modern school) and those of the three other schools. Children of this school were the most rational and objective in their attitudes. They did not focus on control or discipline, did not see the authority figures or the structure of the school as threatening, and were less apt than children of the other schools to be resentful or to conform to the structure of things in a passive and automatic way. This was certainly consistent with their experience in school, where there was considerable attempt to make rules functional and to apply them flexibly, to reduce adult-child distance, and to make children participants in the processes of the classroom.

    In reacting to our questions about right and wrong, fairness, and justice (see Chart 3), the children of our study gave evidence of complex and interesting thinking, with considerable flux and conflict in their ideas. These nine-year-old children were, after all,

    [2] The methods and items described on these charts refer only to material discussed in the presentation; they are selected and condensed from the much wider roster of techniques and measures used in the study.

THE IMPACT OF SCHOOL PHILOSOPHY AND PRACTICE 43

in a transitional stage developmentally. They were emerging from the pervasive parental control of earlier years into a broader world; they faced the conflicting demands of allegiance to adults and to the increasingly important peer group; and they were beginning to move toward the forging of personal and independent codes that would govern their judgments and their behavior in interchange with other people.

Most of these children were past the first stages of moral immaturity, as defined by Piaget and Kohlberg, but there was much variation in their reactions. We might summarize the differences in the school groups as follows:

Children from the traditional schools responded with more constant referral to the school world—its rules, regulations, and infractions (noise, fooling around, poor work, inattention)—and with greater involvement in the consequences that follow transgression. Children of the modern schools, particularly those of Conrad, were less concerned with school infractions and gave more evidence of early attempts to forge principles that transcended adult demands in the school society and had more generalized meaning. Their concepts of the restraints they should ask of themselves were not centered on school mandates for good behavior, and their ideas of a child's misdemeanors were less schoolbound than those of the other children. They evaluated the cheating dilemma in terms of the underlying principle and rejected both conditions as wrong. Children of the other groups were more apt to judge *undetected* cheating as the greater wrong, attaching the magnitude of the transgression to its consequences (in other words, the misdeed is somehow greater if one "gets away with it").

Our findings in this area are somewhat tentative, but they seem to indicate that the Conrad children were moving toward a higher, more advanced stage of moral judgment. Such findings raise an interesting point. They suggest that when a school ties the child sternly to a disciplinary structure—when a school presents the child with the task of keeping constant track of the rules of acceptable behavior—it may defeat its own goal of shaping a morally mature individual. It may hold him longer to a relatively immature level of conscience and evaluation, dominated, in the words of Piaget, by precepts of "adult constraint" and power. When the quality of authority in the school is more flexible and benign, and when the child group is active, powerful, and in constant process of negotiating its own rules for work and play, as it was in Conrad, the child may be moved, even at a young age, to a more

Self-Differentiation

Dictated Letter
(The child was asked to imagine that he had a pen pal in a foreign country to whom he was writing for the first time. He was asked to dictate a letter about himself and his life.)

Stick Figure Scale (10 items)
(The child was asked to describe or evaluate himself by placing himself on a series of continua, the two end points of which were described in contrasting terms, as illustrated in the following example:

"Here's a boy [girl] who's pretty sure all the kids like him, that he's popular." vs. "Here's a boy [girl] who lots of times isn't so sure the other kids like him so much."

Which One Is More Like You?)

Images of Life Stages

Interview Question: "What do you think is the best age to be? Why?"

Stick Figure Scale Item:
"Here's a boy (girl) who thinks it will be wonderful to be all grown up." vs. "Here's a boy (girl) who thinks it was really best when he was a little kid."

Which One Is More Like You?

Children's Picture Story Test
(An adaptation for the age level of the familiar Thematic Apperception Test. It consists of 12 pictures depicting children alone, with other children, in school, and with adults. The child was asked to make up a story for each picture.)

Sentence Completion Item: "The best job in the world would be . . ."

Interview Question: "Have you ever thought about being grown up? What do you think you'll be or do?"

Social Sex Roles

Interview Question: "Do you think it's best to be a boy or girl? Why?"

Stick Figure Scale Item:
"Here's a boy (girl) who thinks boys have the most fun and the best life." vs. "Here's a boy (girl) who thinks girls have the most fun and the best life."

Which One Is More Like You?

Children's Picture Story Test
(see description above)

Play Session
(The child was presented with a wide variety of miniature toys—figures, animals, vehicles, furniture, blocks, etc.—and a large table on which to play out stories with the objects. The session was approximately half an hour.)

Chart 4. Methods and Materials for Study of Children: Self-Differentiation, Images of Life Stages, and Social Sex Roles

generalized plane of thought and judgment about the meaning of behavior and the issues of human interchange.

Children's Self-Image

Now, let us consider our material concerning self-image and the child's sense of identity. We asked a series of questions about possible differences between modern and traditional school children. These questions fall into three subdivisions. First: *self-differentiation*. Would the children differ in self-knowledge? Would they differ in the extent to which their self concepts were differentiated, clear, and personalized? Second: *images of life stages*. Would they differ in their view of their current lives and their growth over time? That is, would they differ in the extent to which they were invested in present or future and in their sense of continuity between different life stages? Third: *social sex roles*. Would they differ in their images of social roles and possibilities—particularly their roles and possibilities as males and females? Would they differ in the extent to which they saw these roles as flexible and permeable, on the one hand, or polarized and set, on the other?

Out of our knowledge of the modern and traditional schools, we predicted that the children of the more modern schools would communicate more differentiated ideas and perceptions about themselves; that they would be more invested in the pleasures and values of the current stage of their lives; and that they would see their own development with more individualized possibilities and with fewer elements of preestablished social roles and limitations. We expected that children of the more traditional schools would describe themselves in more global and impersonal terms; that they would place greater value on the adolescent and adult future as a time of fulfillment, independence, and status; and that they would see their roles as relatively polarized, in sex-typed terms, with preestablished expectations for appropriate behavior and characteristics.

To study these complex ideas, we used a variety of techniques, briefly indicated in Chart 4.

As indicated on the chart, we drew material concerning *self-differentiation* from two sources: a letter to an imaginary pen pal and the Stick Figure Scale. The former was a communication by the child about himself, generated on his own without guidelines. We analyzed these letters in terms of the range and quality of ideas the child conveyed about himself. The Stick Figure Scale presented a series of hypothetical alternatives, describing particular qualities in children, and asking the child to evaluate himself in these terms. There were 10 items, touching on interests, feelings, and self-judgment. We used this test for several purposes, but what is relevant here is the self-differentiation score, in which we assessed the child's subtlety and gradations of judgment, as he matched his own tendencies to the series of illustrative models.

We found that children from the two modern schools included a significantly greater range of qualities, in writing their letters and describing themselves, and were more apt to touch on feelings, plans, memories, and other aspects that went beyond descriptive accounts of their activities. They also responded to the Stick Figure Scale in a more differentiated way, using the possibilities for gradations of judgment with greater variety and flexibility. In all, they communicated a more differentiated and less global image of themselves. In these reactions of the modern school children we may have seen the fused effects of at least two aspects of the modern school: its attempt to teach a probing, differentiated style of thinking in general, and its relatively strong focus on the individual child as the center of his own life and a legitimate object of knowledge.

The child's perspective on *different life stages* was another aspect of self-image we investigated. It seemed to us that the organization and orientation of traditional and modern schools were very different in ways that might well affect the psychological perspective of the children. The traditional schools were preparing the children for the future—training them with the skills and knowledge they would later need. They transmitted images and values concerning the successful adult and offered models they hoped and expected the children would emulate. Where these schools were training children toward established roles and effectiveness in the future, the modern schools were stressing the depth and meaning of the child's current experiences. The modern schools saw past and future as continuous with the present and the child's future development, therefore, as an individual process. This led us to predict that children from traditional environments would be more oriented to the future and that they would project images of the future that were more standardized and had less continuity with their own current experience.

We gathered data in several ways. We asked the children directly about their stage preferences in the interview and in the Stick Figure Scale. We also looked for the prevalence of themes about the future in their projective stories and tapped their images of adult life and the future in the Sentence Completion Test and in the interview.

There were, as predicted, clear differences among the children in their responses to the material. Traditional school children were more apt to think about the future as the time of independence, accomplishment, and arrival. They looked ahead to adolescence and adulthood as preferred life stages. Images of adulthood and the future often took the form of preestablished roles that had no experiential meaning in the present but were conventional and status-oriented: President, secretary, housewife, doctor, banker— or "to go into my father's business"—with no accompanying image of what that business really was.

The modern school pattern was different; it was particularly among the Conrad children that predicted effects of the modern environment appeared. These children were most consistently invested in their current life stage; they were least apt to carry an adult or future orientation into fantasy situations; they were most apt to project a future image developed from the realities of current interests and experiences: to be a puppeteer, dancer, cello player, or "champion swimmer," because these were current hobbies and pleasures, or to search for an occupation that combined their interests ("I like horses and I like to act. I don't know how to combine those two. Maybe in a circus . . . but not really"). This pattern of reaction was particularly striking in its appearance among Conrad girls, since the remaining girls of the sample were even more interested and full of fantasy about the future than the boys were, and often apt to see discontinuous roles waiting for them in that future.

A similar pattern of findings appeared in relation to *social sex roles*. Here we tapped direct attitudes, again, through the interview and Stick Figure Scale (see Chart 4), and we analyzed play sessions and projective stories as a way of assessing the extent to which their fantasies and reactions were sex-typed—that is, typical, in some way, of the reactions and concerns and fantasies that are generally associated with boys rather than girls, or vice versa.

As a word of explanation about this latter point: there are certain conceptions of appropriate male and female behavior that prevail in the culture. Boys, for instance, are allowed and expected to be more aggressive than girls; girls are allowed and expected to be more dependent than boys and more centered on their families. As personality qualities these are considered sex-typed, in the broad culture; and, in fact, considerable research has established over and over that these qualities and themes are associated more with one sex than the other. Allowing for the validity of this prevailing trend, it was still our expectation that the traditional environment fosters a polarization of roles and appropriate qualities more than the modern and that children of the modern schools might thus be less extensively sex-typed in their reactions than children of the traditional schools.

Our findings here were also supportive of the predictions. Most children of this age have some degree of loyalty to their own sex and their own in-group, and some concepts of sex-appropriate role and behavior were absorbed and shared by all the children of our sample. Within this framework, however, there were clear differences of thought and emphasis. The more committed assertions of allegiance to the advantages of one's own sex came from the children of the traditional schools—especially the boys—and these children were characterized also by the more conventional images of role behavior and the more sex-linked themes of play and fantasy. More open attitudes, when they appeared, were generally found among children from modern backgrounds. In this, the girls from modern backgrounds were again notable. They were relatively open in role evaluation, least conventional in their role conceptions, and not apt to typify the dependent, family-centered interests and concerns expected traditionally of girls and actually exemplified by the girls of our study from more traditional backgrounds. In this area, however, we need to note that family home factors were certainly influential, particularly in the role concepts of the girls.

If we were to summarize the findings about modern and traditional school children in terms of developing identity and self-image, we might say that the traditional school children were characterized by more impersonal and global perceptions of themselves as people and by a tendency to look at their own development in terms of the goals and established roles waiting for them and toward which they were being trained. Modern school children were more apt to see themselves, their qualities, and their interests in differentiated terms, to center their energy and attention on their current experiences, and to see their development partly as an individualized evolution out of their current interests and personalities. This pattern characterized the children of Conrad in particular, though some aspects describe the children of both modern schools.

The implications of such differences are many. Some are quite subtle. The risks, problems, and conflicts are not all on one side. It seems to us, however, that these findings are interesting and that they point to important differences in development. They suggest that the impact of the school is indeed broad, going far beyond the academic material it may identify as its curriculum.

It is important, perhaps, to make one last point about our findings. For purposes of this presentation, we have selected some of the study findings that seem pertinent to the conference and that illustrate the extended impact of the school. Even in this context, however, it would be regrettable to leave the impression of a simple and automatic linkage between the nature of a school and the development of all the children who attend it. Our findings have been more differentiated than that, and they have suggested a number of factors that mediate the impact of a school on its children. We have found, for instance, that the pattern of impact will sometimes vary according to the sex of the child. *Boys* from traditional environments, for instance, were particularly assertive about their roles; *girls* from modern environments were particularly open and exploratory in their images of present and future. In a variety of ways, and in many areas of the study, the impact of the schools was filtered not only by the personality of the individual child but by his or her sex membership and experience of life as a boy or girl.

For another thing, the importance of family influence was evident. In our data, it was crucial in some areas, such as the sex role orientation of the girls; in other areas it was less evident. We have many unanswered questions about the interaction of school and home and the effect on a child of family attitudes that support one system of values while the school supports another. What our data *do* suggest is that when the home and school hold consistent orientations, the effect on the child's self-concept and value system is in some way cumulative and particularly powerful.

Yet another factor is the consistency and coherence of the school itself—the extent to which it presents the child with an integrated environment throughout the course of the school day. In the description of the schools, it has been pointed out that Conrad, the most modern, and Browning, the most traditional, presented the most internally coherent environments to the children. When we looked at the children, the clearest contrasts among the four groups were usually between the children of these two schools. Further, the children of Conrad tended toward unique patterns and ideas in various areas of the study. It seems likely that this school created a special impact, at least in part, because of its unified nature as a living and learning environment, the content of its value system, and the fact that it planned school life with conscious expectation that it would have an extensive impact on the child's development.

Implications and Questions

In this study we asked and pursued a broad question: Would schools with different educational philosophies and practices have different effects on developmental processes in the middle years of childhood? To a rather impressive degree the findings were affirmative, although in the area of cognition as measured by problem solving (not reported in this paper), the findings did not follow predicted lines. A search of this kind activates certain broad questions about the impact of school experience which cannot be answered from the findings but which become more differentiated as a result of the research experience. We may have asked these questions before the study began but we ask them differently when the study is over.

We face the question, for instance, of whether it would be possible to trace specific effects to specific aspects of the school environments. To what extent would it be feasible to trace a simple cause-effect route between the mode of authority functioning in school—the way rules are made, who makes them, how flexible they are, how central in the whole scheme of things, and how much obedience has high priority as a virtue—and the children's internalized attitudes toward authority? It seems tenable to posit such a relation. The analysis of the total school environment, however, points to other experiences and relationships not literally tied to the school's discipline system, yet probably potent as influences on the complex phenomenon of attitude toward authority.

One of these is the climate established around knowledge and intellectual mastery. When cognitive experience is thus dealt with non-absolutely, with attention to relativity and to conditioning circumstances, the children are being inducted into a less authoritative mode of thinking which becomes a significant component of their general attitude toward authority. In the modern orientation, knowledge is not straightjacketed into a right-wrong framework; children are introduced early into how altering the perspective, visual or conceptual, can change the face of reality. They are led to consider attenuating circumstance in designating right from wrong and helped to see opinion as an evolutionary process that can move and change as new facts come to light.

In the broad area of interpersonal relationships, apart from the specific systems of regulation and control, there are elements equally relevant to the attitude to authority. How much the children are participants in making decisions, how much they are allowed tasks of important responsibility, how much the distance between adult and child is personalized rather than codified, how much the adult can admit fallibility—all these are factors contributing to the child's way of perceiving authority, to the pattern he builds up for how to feel and how to deal with it, and the image of the kind of authority he will wish to be. Every aspect of interrelationship between teacher and child has meaning as a paradigm for the relation between the powerful and the powerless.

Looked at this way, each of the effects we see associated with either the modern or traditional orientation is multi-determined. We cannot, in this kind of study, arrive at a simple cause-effect line of relation, but we can come closer to understanding the way the constellation of factors interact as determining influences.

In another vein, one asks what happens when we project this study against two major currents in education today: innovations in curriculum geared toward emphasis on cognitive power and changes in method through introduction of technology claiming to support more individualized teaching. The effectiveness of innovations is, in the last analysis, dependent upon the total climate of the school. The use of new techniques will be conditioned by the dominant ideas and values of the institution as well as the motivation and competence of the teacher. A fertile method for stimulating problem-thinking and question-asking, for example, can wither on the vine in an atmosphere where the teachers rely on predefined structured organization and predictable sequences.

There is another complex factor to be considered: the relation between methods and goals. That methods do not have a tenable existence separate from goals is being more widely recognized now than has been true for the past few years—a period during which the surge to update education was most actively expressed in methodological change. But the question of goals is not going to be easily solved. For instance, almost everyone agrees these days on one goal—namely, to individualize education. Yet the agreement is more verbal than real; the concept has diverse, often contradictory meanings. Obviously, the sense in which the modern-oriented schools in our study supported individualized learning has little, if anything, in common with the kind of individualized learning to be accomplished by programmed learning in a computerized system.

In a paper by Oettinger and Marks, the point is made that the latter approach is ultimately valuable for training toward specific behavioral objectives, falling far short of the whole span of educational goals in a changing society. From his perspective as a computer scientist, Oettinger sees these innovations as belonging to an engineering outlook with emphasis on speed, economy, and efficiency. How far they are from the goal of nurturing autonomous individuality is aptly expressed in his statement: "Each pupil is free to go more or less rapidly exactly where he is told to go." [3]

In the last analysis, the place of technology, and the value of educational alternatives in general, must be weighed against the major questions of our times and the broad goals of human development. Young adults, in our day, have presented us with their concern for a society that does not readily offer them experiences and potential for individual fulfillment, and have expressed their wish to influence and change that condition. In evaluating the impact of educational systems we may need to ask what school experiences develop people who can arrive at points of view, as members of their society, through questioning and analysis, and who are motivated to make things happen in new and imaginative ways. The differences we have found between modern and traditional schools may be relevant to such goals and concepts.

[3] A. Oettinger and S. Marks. "Educational Technology: New Myths and Old Realities." *Harvard Educational Review* 38 (4): 701; Fall 1968.

Teacher Expectation and Pupil Learning[1]

ROBERT ROSENTHAL

THE primary purpose of this paper is to consider the proposition that a teacher's expectation about his pupil's performance can come to serve as a significant determinant of that performance. Later in this paper we shall examine the evidence for and some implications of this proposition, but first we shall want to provide an appropriate historical and conceptual perspective. The goal of this perspective is to show that there is, in fact, nothing very special about the "effects of teacher expectations." These effects may be seen to be only a specific instance of the operation of a far more general principle. This principle holds that often in the course of interpersonal relationships, one person's expectation for the behavior of another person can come to be a significant determinant of that other person's behavior.

Most of the systematic evidence to support the idea of what we may call interpersonal self-fulfilling prophecies comes from experiments conducted not with teachers but with psychological experimenters. Simply to extend the generality of the principle of interpersonal self-fulfilling prophecies, any other group of persons might

[1] Preparation of this chapter and much of the research summarized here was supported by research grants (G-17685, G-24826, GS-177, GS-714, and GS-1741) from the Division of Social Sciences of the National Science Foundation. Much of the research summarized here has also been summarized elsewhere but in the context of a more technical exposition (Rosenthal, 1969). Readers interested in the more technical details of the experiments summarized only briefly in the present chapter will want to refer to the more extensive bibliography of that paper.

have served equally well. But the social situation which comes into being when a behavioral scientist encounters his research subject is a situation of both general and unique importance to the field of education and to the other behavioral sciences. Its general importance derives from the fact that the interaction of experimenter and subject, like other hierarchically ordered two-person interactions, may be investigated empirically with a view to teaching us more about such dyadic interaction in general. Its unique importance derives from the fact that the interaction of experimenter and subject, unlike other dyadic interactions, is a major source of knowledge in the field of education and in the other behavioral sciences.

Experimenter Expectations

The particular expectation a scientist has of how his experiment will turn out is variable, depending on the experiment being conducted, but the presence of some expectation is virtually a constant in science. The variables selected for study by the scientist are not chosen by means of a table of random numbers. They are selected because the scientist expects a certain relationship to appear among them. Even in those less carefully planned examinations of relationships called "fishing expeditions," or more formally, "exploratory analyses," the expectation of the scientist is reflected in the selection of the entire set of variables chosen for examination. Exploratory analyses of data, like real fishing ventures, do not take place in randomly selected pools.

These expectations of the scientist are likely to affect the choice of the experimental design and procedure in such a way as to increase the likelihood that his expectation or hypothesis will be supported. That is as it should be. No scientist would select intentionally a procedure likely to show his hypothesis in error. If he could too easily think of procedures that would show this, he would be likely to revise his hypothesis. If the selection of a research design or procedure is regarded by another scientist as too "biased" to be a fair test of the hypothesis, he can test the hypothesis employing oppositely biased procedures or less biased procedures by which to demonstrate the greater value of his hypothesis. The designs and procedures employed are, to a great extent, public knowledge, and it is this public character that permits relevant replications to serve the required corrective function.

The major concern of this section will be with the effects of the experimenter's expectation on the responses he obtains from his subjects. The consequences of such an expectancy bias can be quite serious. Expectancy effects on subjects' responses are not public matters. It is not only that other scientists cannot know whether such effects occurred in the experimenter's interaction with his subjects, but the investigator himself may not know whether these effects have occurred. Moreover, there is the likelihood that the experimenter has not even considered the possibility of such unintended effects on his subject's response. This is not so different from the situations wherein the subject's response is affected by any attribute of the experimenter. Later, the problem will be discussed in more detail. For now it is enough to note that while other attributes of the experimenter may affect the subject's response, they do not necessarily affect these responses differentially as a function of the subject's treatment condition. Expectancy effects, on the other hand, always do. The sex of the experimenter does not change as a function of the subject's treatment condition in an experiment. The experimenter's expectancy of how the subject will respond does change as a function of the subject's experimental treatment condition.

That one person's expectation about another person's behavior may contribute to a determination of what that behavior will actually be has been suggested by various theorists. Merton (1948) elaborated the very useful concept of "self-fulfilling prophecy." One prophesies an event and the expectation of the event, then changes the behavior of the prophet in such a way as to make the prophesied event more likely. The late Gordon Allport (1950) applied the concept of interpersonal expectancies to an analysis of the causes of war. Nations expecting to go to war affect the behavior of their opponents-to-be by the behavior which reflects their expectations of armed conflict. Nations who expect to remain out of wars at least sometimes manage to avoid entering into them.

Drawn from the general literature, and the literatures of the healing professions, survey research, and laboratory psychology, there is considerable suggestive evidence for the operation of interpersonal self-fulfilling prophecies. The literatures referred to have been reviewed elsewhere (Rosenthal, 1964a, 1964b, 1965, 1966; Rosenthal and Jacobson, 1968), but it may be of interest here to give one illustration from the literature of experimental psychology. The case is one known generally to psychologists as a case study of an artifact in animal research. It is less well known, however, as a case study of the effect of experimenter expectancy. While the subject sample was small, the experimenter sample was very large indeed. The case, of course, is that of Clever Hans (Pfungst, 1911). Hans, it will be remembered, was the horse of Mr. von Osten, a German mathematics teacher. By means of tapping his foot, Hans was able to add, subtract, multiply, and divide. Hans could spell, read, and solve problems of musical harmony. To be sure, there were other clever animals at the time, and Pfungst tells about them. There was "Rosa," the mare of Berlin, who performed similar feats in vaudeville; and there was the dog of Utrecht; and the reading pig of Virginia. All these other clever animals were highly trained performers who were, of course, intentionally cued by their trainers.

Mr. von Osten, however, did not profit from his animal's talent, nor did it seem at all likely that he was attempting to perpetrate a fraud. He swore he did not cue the animal, and he permitted other people to question and test the horse even without his being present. Pfungst and his famous colleague, Stumpf, undertook a program of systematic research to discover the secret of Hans' talents. Among the first discoveries made was that if the horse could not see the questioner, Hans was not clever at all. Similarly, if the questioner did not himself know the answer to the question, Hans could not answer it either. Still, Hans was able to answer Pfungst's questions as long as the investigator was present and visible.

Pfungst reasoned that the questioner might in some way be signaling to Hans when to begin and when to stop tapping his foot. A forward inclination of the head of the questioner would start Hans tapping, Pfungst observed. He tried then to incline his head forward without asking a question and discovered that this was sufficient to start Hans' tapping. As the experimenter straightened up, Hans would stop tapping.

Pfungst then tried to get Hans to stop tapping by using very slight upward motions of the head. He found that even the raising of his eyebrows was sufficient. Even the dilation of the questioner's nostrils was a cue for Hans to stop tapping.

When the questioner bent forward more, the horse would tap faster. This added to the reputation of Hans as brilliant. That is, when a large number of taps was the correct response, Hans would tap very, very rapidly until he approached the region of correctness, and then he began to slow down. It was found that questioners typically bent forward more when the answer was a long one, gradually straightening up as Hans got closer to the correct number.

For some experiments, Pfungst discovered that auditory cues functioned additively with visual cues. When the experimenter was silent, Hans was able to respond correctly 31 percent of the time in picking one of many placards with different words written on them, or cloths of different colors. When auditory cues were added, Hans responded correctly 56 percent of the time.

Pfungst himself then played the part of Hans, tapping out responses to questions with his hand. Of 25 questioners, 23 unwittingly cued Pfungst as to when to stop tapping in order to give a correct response. None of the questioners (males and females of all ages and occupations) knew the intent of the experiment. When errors occurred, they were usually only a single tap from being correct. The subjects of this study, including an experienced psychologist, were unable to discover that they were unintentionally emitting cues.

Hans' amazing talents, talents rapidly acquired too by Pfungst, serve to illustrate the power of the self-fulfilling prophecy. Hans' questioners, even skeptical ones, expected Hans to give the correct answers to their queries. Their expectation was reflected in their unwitting signal to Hans that the time had come for him to stop his tapping. The signal cued Hans to stop, and the questioner's expectation became the reason for Hans' being, once again, correct.

Not all of Hans' questioners were equally good at fulfilling their prophecies. Even when the subject is a horse, apparently, the attributes of the experimenter make a considerable difference in determining the response of a subject. On the basis of his studies, Pfungst was able to summarize the characteristics of those of Hans' questioners who were more successful in their covert and unwitting communication with the horse. Among the characteristics of the more successful unintentional influencers were those of tact, an air of dominance, attention to the business at hand, and a facility for motor discharge. Pfungst's observations of 60 years ago seem not to have suffered excessively from the lack of more modern methods of scaling observations. To anticipate some of the research findings turned up much later, it must be said that Pfungst's description seems also to fit those experimenters who are more likely to affect their human subjects' responses by virtue of their experimental hypothesis.

In summarizing his difficulties in learning the nature of Clever Hans' talents, Pfungst felt that he had been too long off the track by "looking for in the horse, what should have been sought in the man." Perhaps, too, when we conduct research in the behavioral sciences we are sometimes caught looking at our subjects when we ought to be looking at ourselves. It was to this possibility that much of the research to be summarized here was addressed.

Animal Learning

A good beginning might have been to replicate Pfungst's research, but with horses hard to come by, rats were made to do (Rosenthal and Fode, 1963a).

A class in experimental psychology had been performing experiments with human subjects for most of a semester. Now they were asked to perform one more experiment, the last in the course, and the first employing animal subjects. The experimenters were told of studies that had shown that maze-brightness and maze-dullness could be developed in strains of rats by successive inbreeding of the well- and the poorly-performing maze-runners. Sixty laboratory rats were equitably divided among the 12 experimenters. Half the experimenters were told that their rats were maze-bright while the other half were told their rats were maze-dull. The animal's task was to learn to run to the darker of two arms of an elevated T-maze. The two arms of the maze, one white and one gray, were interchangeable; and the "correct" or rewarded arm was equally often on the right as on the left. Whenever an animal ran to the correct side he obtained a food reward. Each rat was given 10 trials each day for five days to learn that the darker side of the maze was the one which led to the food.

Beginning with the first day and continuing throughout the experiment, animals believed to be better performers became better performers. Animals believed to be brighter showed a daily improvement in their performance, while those believed to be dull improved only to the third day and then showed a worsening of performance. Sometimes an animal refused to budge from his starting position. This happened 11 percent of the time among the allegedly bright rats; but among allegedly dull rats it happened 29 percent of the time. When animals did respond and correctly so, those believed to be brighter ran faster to the rewarded side of the maze than did even the correctly responding rats believed to be dull.

When the experiment was over, all experimenters made ratings of their rats and of their own attitudes and behavior vis-à-vis their animals. Those experimenters who had been led to expect better performance viewed their animals as brighter, more pleasant, and more likable. These same experimenters felt more relaxed in their contacts with the animals and described their behavior toward them as more pleasant, friendly, enthusiastic, and less talkative. They also stated that they handled their rats more and also more gently than did the experimenters expecting poor performance.

So far we have given only one example of the results of studies of expectancy effect and the subjects were animals. Most of the research available, however, is based on human subjects and it is those results we now consider. In this set of experiments at least 20 different specific tasks have been employed, but some of these tasks seemed sufficiently related to one another that they could reasonably be regarded as a family of tasks or a research area. These areas include human abilities, psychophysical judgments, reaction time, inkblot tests, structured laboratory interviews, and person perception. We have space, however, only to consider some examples.

Human Abilities

Especially instructive for its unusual within-subject experimental manipulation was an experiment by Larrabee and Kleinsasser (1967). They employed five experimenters to administer the Wechsler Intelligence Scale for Children (WISC) to 12 sixth graders of average intelligence. Each subject was tested by two different experimenters; one administering the even-numbered items and the other administering the odd-numbered items. For each subject, one of the experimenters was told the child was of above average intelligence while the other experimenter was told the child was of below average intelligence. When the child's experimenter expected superior performance the total IQ earned was over 7 points higher on the average than when the child's experimenter expected inferior performance. When only the performance subtests of the WISC were considered, the advantage to the children of having been expected to do well was less than three IQ points and could easily have occurred by chance. When only the verbal subtests of the WISC were considered, however, the advantage of having been expected to do well exceeded 10 IQ points. The particular subtest most affected by experimenters' expectancies was Information. The results of this study are especially striking in view of the very small sample size (12) of subjects employed.

The other experiment to be mentioned in this section is of special importance because of the elimination of plausible alternatives to the hypothesis that it is the subject's response that is affected by the experimenter's expectancy. In his experiment, Johnson (1967) employed the Stevenson marble-dropping task. Each of the 20 experimenters was led to believe that marble-dropping rate was related to intelligence. More intelligent subjects were alleged to show a greater increase in rate of marble-dropping over the course of six trials. Each experimenter then contacted eight subjects, half of whom were alleged to be brighter than the remaining subjects.

The recording of the subject's response was by means of an electric counter and the counter was read by the investigator who was blind to the subject's expectancy condition. The results of this study, one of the best controlled in this area, were the most dramatic. Experimenters expecting a greater increase in marble-dropping rate obtained a much greater increase than they did when expecting a lesser increase.

Inkblot Tests

In one of the most recent of the inkblot experiments, Marwit (1968) employed 20 graduate students in clinical psychology as his experimenters and 40 undergraduate students of introductory psychology as his subjects. Half the experimenters were led to expect some of their subjects to give many Rorschach responses and, especially, a lot of animal responses. Half the experimenters were led to expect some of their subjects to give few Rorschach responses but proportionately a lot of human responses. Results showed that subjects who were expected to give more responses gave more responses and that subjects who were expected to give a greater number of animal relative to human responses did so. Marwit also found trends for the first few responses to have been already affected by the experimenter's expectancy and for later-contacted subjects to show greater effects of experimenter expectancy than earlier-contacted subjects.

Structured Laboratory Interviews

A number of experiments have been carried out in which the experimenters conducted a structured interview with their research subjects. One of these, an experiment by Raffetto (1968), was addressed to the question of whether the experimenter's expectation for greater reports of hallucinatory behavior might be a significant determinant of such reports.

Raffetto employed 96 paid, female students from a variety of less advanced undergraduate courses to participate in an experiment on sensory restriction. Subjects were asked to spend one hour in a small room that was relatively quite free from light and sound. Eight more advanced students of psychology served as the experimenters, with each one interviewing 12 of the subjects before and after the sensory restriction experience. The pre-experimental interview consisted of factual questions such as age, college major, and college grades. The post-experimental interview was relatively well-structured, including questions to be answered by "yes" or "no" as well as more open-ended questions, for example, "Did you notice any particular sensations or feelings?" Post-experimental interviews were tape recorded.

Half the experimenters were led to expect high reports of hallucinatory experiences and half were led to expect low reports of hallucinatory experiences. Obtained scores of hallucinatory experiences ranged from zero to 32 with a grand mean of 5.4. Of the subjects contacted by experimenters expecting more hallucinatory experiences, 48 percent were scored above the mean on these experiences. Of the subjects contacted by experimenters expecting fewer hallucinatory experiences, only 6 percent were scored above the mean.

Person Perception

Although a good many experiments on the effects of experimenter expectancy have been conducted in the area of person perception, the basic paradigm of these investigations has been sufficiently uniform that we need only an illustration (Rosenthal and Fode, 1963b).

Ten advanced undergraduates and graduate students of psychology served as the experimenters. All were enrolled in an advanced course in experimental psychology and were already involved in conducting research. Each student-experimenter was assigned as his subjects a group of about 20 students of introductory psychology. The experimental procedure was for the experimenter to show a series of 10 photographs of people's faces to each of his subjects individually. The subject was to rate the degree of success or failure shown in the face of each person pictured in the photos. Each face could be rated as any value from -10 to $+10$, with -10 meaning extreme failure and $+10$ meaning extreme success. The 10 photos had been selected so that, on the average, they would be seen as neither successful nor unsuccessful, but quite neutral, with an average numerical score of zero.

All 10 experimenters were given identical instructions on how to administer the task to their subjects and were given identical instructions to read to their subjects. They were cautioned not to deviate from these instructions. The purpose of their participation, it was explained to all experimenters, was to see how well they could duplicate experimental results which were already well-established. Half the experimenters were told that the "well-established" finding was such that their subjects should rate the photos as of successful people (ratings of +5) and half the experimenters were told that their subjects should rate the photos as being of unsuccessful people (ratings of −5). Results showed that experimenters expecting higher photo ratings obtained higher photo ratings than did experimenters expecting lower photo ratings.

Subsequent experiments in the program of research launched with the experiment just described were designed not so much to demonstrate the effects of the investigator's expectancy as to learn something about the conditions which increase, decrease, or otherwise modify these effects. It was learned, for example, that the subject's expectations about what would constitute behavior appropriate to the role of "experimental subject" could alter the extent to which they were influenced by the effects of the experimenter's hypothesis.

Through the employment of accomplices, serving as the first few subjects, it was learned that when the responses of the first few subjects confirmed the experimenter's hypothesis, his behavior toward his subsequent subjects was affected in such a way that these subjects tended to confirm further the experimenter's hypothesis. When accomplices, serving as the first few subjects, intentionally disconfirmed the expectation of the experimenter, the real subjects subsequently contacted were affected by a change in the experimenter's behavior so as also to disconfirm his experimental hypothesis. It seems possible, then, that the results of behavioral research can, by virtue of the early data returns, be determined by the performance of just the first few subjects.

In some of the experiments conducted, it was found that when experimenters were offered a too-large and a too-obvious incentive to affect the results of their research, the effects of expectancy tended to diminish. It speaks well for the integrity of our student-experimenters that when they felt bribed to get the data we led them to expect, they seemed actively to oppose us. There was a tendency for those experimenters to "bend over backward" to avoid the biasing effects of their expectation, but with the bending so far backward that the results of their experiments tended to be significantly opposite to the results they had been led to expect.

Individual differences among experimenters in the degree to

which they obtain results consistent with their hypothesis have been discovered. The evidence comes both from additional experiments and from the analysis of sound motion pictures of experimenters interacting with their experimental subjects. Those experimenters who show greater expectancy effects tend to be of higher status in the eyes of their subjects and they seem to conduct their experiments in a more professional, more competent manner. They are judged more likable and more relaxed, particularly in their movement patterns, while avoiding an overly personal tone of voice that might interfere with the business at hand. It is interesting to note that, although the influence of an experimenter's expectancy is quite unintentional, the characteristics of the more successful influencer are very much the same ones associated with more effective influencers when the influence is intentional. The more successful agent of social influence may be the same person, whether the influence be as overt and intentional as in the case of outright persuasion attempts, or as covert and unintentional as in the case of the experimenter's subtly communicating his expectancy to his research subject.

Experimenter Expectations: A Summary

There have been 103 experiments testing the effects on subjects' responses of their experimenter's expectations and these studies can be classified into seven different research domains. Table 1 shows the number of studies conducted in each of these seven areas and the percentage of the studies in each area obtaining results with an associated probability of 10 percent or less. Table 1 also shows the number of principal investigators who conducted one or more studies in each of the seven areas and the percentage of these investigators in each area who obtained results with an associated p of 10 percent or less. By chance we expect only about 10 percent of the experiments or the investigators to obtain results "significant" at the 10 percent level. In fact, we find about five times that number of experiments or investigators obtaining results at that level. The probability of this many positive results occurring by chance is infinitely small.

Because so much of the business of the behavioral sciences is transacted at a number of particular levels of probability, an additional summary is provided. Table 2 shows for 103 experiments, for 52 investigators, and for 33 laboratories (see Appendix A), the percentage obtaining results at five different levels of p.

	By Experiments		By Investigators	
Research Area	Number of Studies	Percentage of Studies at $p \leq .10$ [d]	Number of Investigators	Percentage of Studies at $p \leq .10$ [d]
Animal Learning	9	100%	5	100%
Human Abilities [a]	10	40%	9	44%
Psychophysics [a]	9	33%	6	33%
Reaction Time	3	67%	3	67%
Inkblot Tests	5	80%	4	75%
Laboratory Interviews [b]	6	83%	6	83%
Person Perception [a,b]	64	36%	22	27%
Total [c]	103	48%	52	50%

[a] Indicates a single experiment or investigator represented in each of three areas by the same subject sample.

[b] Indicates another experiment or investigator represented in two areas by the same subject sample.

[c] Three entries were non-independent with respect to their subject samples, and the mean standard normal deviate across areas was computed to obtain the independent p level entries.

[d] One-tail.

Table 1. Experimenter Expectancy Effects in Seven Research Areas

p (one-tail)	I Experiments	II Investigators [a]	III Laboratories
$< .10$	48%	50%	58%
$< .05$	34%	37%	48%
$< .01$	17%	27%	36%
$< .001$	12%	19%	27%
$< .0001$	5%	10%	18%
N	103	52	33
$\dfrac{\text{Grand Sum } z}{\sqrt{\text{Number of units}}}$	$\dfrac{+100.86}{\sqrt{103}}$	$\dfrac{+69.75}{\sqrt{52}}$	$\dfrac{+57.86}{\sqrt{33}}$
Combined z [b]	+ 9.94	+ 9.67	+10.08
Null Replicates [c]	3,656	1,746	1,204

[a] Principal investigators may be represented in more than one research area. Entries in Column III, however, are entirely independent with type of research area disregarded.

[b] Standard normal deviate associated with overall p for experiments, investigators, and laboratories.

[c] Number of additional experiments, investigators, and laboratories obtaining perfectly null results ($z = 0.00$, exactly) required to bring overall combined p to .05.

Table 2. Experimenter Expectancy Effects Obtained at Various p Levels

Tables 1 and 2 tell us that the effects of experimenters' expectancies are "real" but they do not tell us whether they are large in magnitude in a given experiment. On the basis of analyses reported elsewhere (Rosenthal, 1969), it can be estimated that about two out of three research subjects and about two out of three experimenters will give or obtain responses in the direction of the experimenter's expectancy.

Though we have been able to arrive at some estimate, however crude, of the magnitude of expectancy effects, we will not know quite how to assess this magnitude until we have comparative estimates from other areas of behavioral research. Such estimates are not easy to come by, but it seems worthwhile for us to try to obtain such estimates in the future. Although in individual studies, investigators occasionally give the proportion of variance accounted for by their experimental variable, it is rarer that systematic reviews of bodies of research literature give estimates of the overall magnitude of effects of the variable under consideration. It does not seem an unreasonable guess, however, to suggest that in the bulk of the experimental literature of the behavioral sciences, the effects of the experimental variable are not impressively "larger," either in the sense of magnitude of obtained p's or in the sense of proportion of subjects affected, than the effects of experimenter expectancy. The best support for such an assertion would come from experiments in which the effects of experimenter expectancy are compared directly, in the same experiment, with the effects of some other experimental variable believed to be a significant determinant of behavior. Fortunately, there are two such experiments to shed light on the question.

The first of these was conducted by Burnham (1966). He had 23 experimenters each run one rat in a T-maze discrimination problem. About half the rats had been lesioned by removal of portions of the brain, and the remaining animals had received only sham surgery which involved cutting through the skull but no damage to brain tissue. The purpose of the study was explained to the experimenters as an attempt to learn the effects of lesions on discrimination learning. Expectancies were manipulated by labeling each rat as lesioned or nonlesioned. Some of the really lesioned rats were labeled accurately as lesioned but some were falsely labeled as unlesioned. Some of the really unlesioned rats were labeled accurately as unlesioned but some were falsely labeled as lesioned. The results showed that animals that had been lesioned did not perform as well as those that had not been lesioned and animals that were believed to be lesioned did not perform as well as those that were believed to be unlesioned. What makes this experiment of special interest is that the effects of experimenter expectancy were actually greater than the effects of the removal of brain tissue.

The first of the experiments to compare directly the effects of experimenter expectancy with some other experimental variable employed animal subjects. The next such experiment to be described employed human subjects. Cooper, Eisenberg, Robert, and Dohrenwend (1967) wanted to compare the effects of experimenter expectancy with the effects of effortful preparation for an examination on the degree of belief that the examination would actually take place.

Each of 10 experimenters contacted 10 subjects; half of the subjects were required to memorize a list of 16 symbols and definitions that were claimed to be essential to the taking of a test that had a 50-50 chance of being given, while the remaining subjects, the "low effort" group, were asked only to look over the list of symbols. Half of the experimenters were led to expect that "high effort" subjects would be more certain of actually having to take the test, while half of the experimenters were led to expect that "low effort" subjects would be more certain of actually having to take the test.

Results showed that there was a very slight tendency for subjects who had exerted greater effort to believe more strongly that they would be taking the test. Surprising in its magnitude was the finding that experimenters expecting to obtain responses of greater certainty obtained such responses to a much greater degree than did experimenters expecting responses of lesser certainty. The effects of the experimenters' expectancies were more than 10 times greater than the effects of preparatory effort.

Experimenter Expectations: Mediating Processes

How are we to account for the results of the experiments described? What are the processes by which an experimenter unintentionally informs his subject just what response is expected of him?

We know that the process whereby the experimenter communicates his expectancy to his subject is a subtle one. We know that it is subtle because for six years we have tried to find in sound films the unintended cues the experimenter gives the subject—and for six years we have failed, at least partly. Yet there are some things about the unintentional communication of expectancies that have been learned.

We know that, if a screen is placed between experimenter and subject, there will be a reduction of the expectancy effect so that visual cues from the experimenter are probably important (Rosenthal and Fode, 1963; Zoble, 1968). But the interposed screen does not eliminate expectancy effects completely, so that auditory cues also seem to be important. Just how important auditory cues may be has been dramatically demonstrated by the work of Adair and Epstein (1968). They first conducted a study which was essentially a replication of the basic experiment on the self-fulfilling effects of experimenters' prophecies. Results showed that, just as in the original studies, experimenters who prophesied the perception of success by their subjects fulfilled their prophecies, as did the experimenters who had prophesied the perception of failure by their subjects.

During the conduct of this replication experiment, Adair and Epstein tape-recorded the experimenters' instructions to their subjects. The second experiment was then conducted not by experimenters at all, but by tape recordings of experimenters' voices reading standard instructions to their subjects. When the tape-recorded instructions had originally been read by experimenters expecting success perception by their subjects, the tape recordings evoked greater success perceptions from their subjects. When the tape-recorded instructions had originally been read by experimenters expecting failure perception by their subjects, the tape recordings evoked greater failure perceptions from their subjects. Self-fulfilling prophecies, it seems, can come about as a result of the prophet's voice alone. Since, in the experiment described, all prophets read standard instructions, self-fulfillment of prophecies may be brought about by the tone in which the prophet prophesies.

Early in the history of the research program on self-fulfilling prophecies in the behavioral sciences, it had been thought that a process of operant conditioning might be responsible for their operation (Rosenthal, 1966). It was thought that perhaps every time the subject gave a response consistent with the experimenter's expectancy, the experimenter might look more pleasant, or smile, or glance at the subject approvingly, even without the experimenter's being aware of his own reinforcing responses. The experimenter, in other words, might unwittingly have taught the subject what responses were the desired ones. Several experiments were analyzed to see whether this hypothesis of operant conditioning might apply.

If it did apply, we would expect that the subjects' responses gradually would become more like those prophesied by the experimenter—that there would be a learning curve for subjects, but no learning curve was found. On the contrary, it turned out that the subjects' very first responses were about as much affected by their experimenters' expectancies as were their very last responses. Since the very first response, by definition, cannot follow any unwitting reinforcement by the experimenter, the mechanism of operant conditioning can be ruled out as necessary to the communication of experimenters' expectancies.

True, there was no learning curve for subjects, but there seemed to be a learning curve for experimenters. Several studies showed that expected results became more likely as more subjects were contacted by each experimenter (Rosenthal, 1966; 1969). In fact, there was very little expectancy effect in evidence for just the very first-seen subjects. If the experimenter were indeed learning to increase the unintended influence of his prophecy, who would be the teacher? Probably the subject. It seems reasonable to think of a subject's responding in the direction of the experimenter's hypothesis as a reinforcing event. Therefore, whatever the covert communicative behavior of the experimenter that preceded the subject's reinforcement, it will be more likely to recur. Subjects, then, may quite unintentionally shape the experimenter's unintended communicative behavior. Not only does the experimenter influence his subjects to respond in the expected manner, but his subjects may well evoke just that unintended behavior that will lead them to respond increasingly as prophesied. Probably neither subject nor experimenter "knows" just exactly what the unintended communication behavior is—and neither do we.

Experimenter Expectations: Methodological Implications

The implications of the research on the effects of the experimenter's expectancy on the results of his research are of two general kinds: those that are primarily methodological and those that are more substantive. Our focus in this paper is more on some of the substantive implications, but brief mention may be made of some implications for how we conduct research in the behavioral sciences.

To the extent that the results of behavioral research are affected by the expectation of the experimenter, we can only place a lessened confidence in these results. But to say that our confidence is weakened in the results of many experiments as they are actually conducted is not to say that our confidence is weakened in the basic logic of the experimental method. We must simply take those, only sometimes inconvenient, extra precautions required to prevent or reduce expectancy effects or those procedures designed to permit us to assess whether they have or have not affected the results of our research.

It is possible for research investigators to employ, as data collectors, research assistants who have not been told the purpose of the research. As long as the investigator's expectation can be kept from these data collectors, there should be no effects attributable to the investigator's expectation. There are some experiments in which the experimenter need have no direct contact with the subjects and, in such studies, automated data collection systems should be employed to reduce any possibility of the unintended influence of the experimenter's expectation. When a human data collector is required, and that is often the case, at least the amount of contact between experimenter and subject can be reduced in order to minimize any opportunity for unintended communication.

Not only because of the danger of expectancy effects but also because of the general nature of other experimenter effects, it would be desirable to employ larger numbers of experimenters for each study than are now routinely employed. That would permit the assessment of the extent to which different experimenters obtained different results and, in any area of psychological research, that is a fact worth knowing.

Only one final technique for the control of expectancy effects can be mentioned here and that is the employment of special control groups known as "expectancy controls." In any experiment employing an experimental (treatment) and a control (no treatment) condition, two extra groups are added. In one of these added groups, the data collector is led to believe that no treatment has been administered when, in fact, it has. In the other added group, the data collector is led to believe that the treatment has been administered when, in fact, it has not. Such a research design permits the assessment of the effects in which the investigator is primarily interested as well as the assessment of the magnitude or complicating effect of the experimenter's expectancy (Rosenthal, 1966). It may be noted that the important studies by Burnham (1966) and by Cooper et al. (1967), both described earlier, were the first to employ this basic research paradigm.

Most of what has been said so far may seem to be not very directly related to the title of this paper and of this section. Yet what has been said is a necessary introduction, designed to emphasize that there is nothing very special about the idea that a teacher's expectation about her pupils' performance can come to serve as a partial determinant of those pupils' performance. If rats can become brighter when expected to by their experimenter, it can hardly be thought to be farfetched to suppose that children could also become brighter when expected to by their teacher. Kenneth Clark (1963), in any case, has presented the view for some time that culturally disadvantaged children are the unfortunate victims of teachers' educational self-fulfilling prophecies. The following experiment, then, was simply an extension of the earlier work on interpersonal expectations (Rosenthal and Jacobson, 1968).

Teacher Expectations

All of the children in an elementary school serving a lower socioeconomic status neighborhood were administered a nonverbal test of intelligence. The test was disguised as one that would predict intellectual "blooming." There were 18 classrooms in the school, three at each of the six grade levels. Within each grade level the three classrooms were composed of children with above average ability, average ability, and below average ability, respectively. Within each of the 18 classrooms, approximately 20 percent of the children were chosen at random to form the experimental group. Each teacher was given the names of the children from her class who were in the experimental condition. The teacher was told that these children had scored on the "test for intellectual blooming" such that they would show remarkable gains in intellectual competence during the next eight months of school. The difference between the experimental group and the control group children, then, was in the mind of the teacher.

At the end of the school year, eight months later, all the children were retested with the same IQ test. This intelligence test, while relatively nonverbal in the sense of requiring no speaking, reading, or writing, was not entirely nonverbal. Actually there were two subtests, one requiring a greater comprehension of English—a kind of picture vocabulary test. The other subtest required less ability to understand any spoken language but more ability to reason abstractly. For shorthand purposes we refer to the former as a "verbal" subtest and to the latter as a "reasoning" subtest. The pretest correlation between these subtests was +.42.

For the school as a whole, the children of the experimental

group showed only a slightly greater gain in verbal IQ (2 points) than did the control group children. However, in total IQ (4 points) and especially in reasoning IQ (7 points), the experimental group children gained appreciably more than did the control group children.

When educational theorists have discussed the possible effects of teachers' expectations, they have usually referred to the children at lower levels of scholastic achievement. It was interesting, therefore, to find that in the present study, children of the highest level of achievement showed as great a benefit as did the children of the lowest level of achievement of having their teachers expect intellectual gains.

At the end of the school year of this study, all teachers were asked to describe the classroom behavior of their pupils. Those children from whom intellectual growth was expected were described as having a significantly better chance of becoming successful in the future, as significantly more interesting, curious, and happy.

There was a tendency, too, for these children to be seen as more appealing, adjusted, and affectionate and as lower in the need for social approval. In short, the children from whom intellectual growth was expected became more intellectually alive and autonomous or at least were so perceived by their teachers.

We have already seen that the children of the experimental group gained more intellectually, so that perhaps it was the fact of such gaining that accounted for the more favorable ratings of these children's behavior and aptitude. But a great many of the control group children also gained in IQ during the course of the year. We might expect that those who gained more intellectually among these undesignated children would also be rated more favorably by their teachers. Such was not the case. The more the control group children gained in IQ the more they were regarded as less well-adjusted, as less interesting, and as less affectionate.

From these results it would seem that when children who are expected to grow intellectually do so, they are considerably benefited in other ways as well. When children who are not especially expected to develop intellectually do so, they seem either to show accompanying undesirable behavior or at least are perceived by their teachers as showing such undesirable behavior. If a child is to show intellectual gain, it seems to be better for his real or perceived intellectual vitality and for his real or perceived mental health if his teacher has been expecting him to grow intellectually.

It appears worthwhile to investigate further the proposition that there may be hazards to unpredicted intellectual growth.

A closer analysis of these data, broken down by whether the children were in the high, medium, or low ability tracks or groups, showed that these effects of unpredicted intellectual growth were due primarily to the children of the low ability group. When these slow track children were in the control group so that no intellectual gains were expected of them, they were rated more unfavorably by their teachers if they did show gains in IQ. The greater their IQ gains, the more unfavorably were they rated, both as to mental health and as to intellectual vitality. Even when the slow track children were in the experimental group, so that IQ gains were expected of them, they were not rated as favorably relative to their control group peers as were the children of the high or medium track, despite the fact that they gained as much in IQ relative to the control group children as did the experimental group children of the high group. It may be difficult for a slow track child, even one whose IQ is rising, to be seen by his teacher as a well-adjusted child, and as a potentially successful child, intellectually.

The effects of teacher expectations had been most dramatic when measured in terms of pupils' gains in reasoning IQ. These effects on reasoning IQ, however, were not uniform for boys and girls. Although all the children of this lower socioeconomic status school gained dramatically in IQ, it was only among the girls that greater gains were shown by those who were expected to bloom compared to the children of the control group. Among the boys, those who were expected to bloom gained less than did the children of the control group.

In part to check this finding, the experiment originally conducted on the West Coast was repeated in a small Midwestern town (Rosenthal and Evans, 1968). This time the children were from substantial middle-class backgrounds, and this time the results were completely and significantly reversed. Now it was the boys who showed the benefits of favorable teacher expectations. Among the girls, those who were expected to bloom intellectually gained less in reasoning IQ than did the girls of the control group. Just as in the West Coast experiment, however, all the children showed substantial gains in IQ. These results, while they suggest the potentially powerful effects of teacher expectations, also indicate the probable complexity of these effects as a function of pupils' sex, social class, and, as time will no doubt show, other variables as well.

In both the experiments described, IQ gains were assessed after a full academic year had elapsed. However, the results of another experiment suggest that teacher expectations can significantly affect students' intellectual performance in a period as short as two months (Anderson and Rosenthal, 1968). In this small experiment, the 25 children were mentally retarded boys with an average pretest IQ of 46. Expectancy effects were significant only for reasoning IQ and only in interaction with membership in a group receiving special remedial reading instruction in addition to participating in the school's summer day camp program. Among these specially tutored boys, those who were expected to bloom showed an expectancy disadvantage of nearly 12 IQ points; among the untutored boys who were participating only in the school's summer day camp program, those who were expected to bloom showed an expectancy advantage of just over three IQ points. (For verbal IQ, in contrast, the expectancy disadvantage of the tutored boys was less than one IQ point, while the expectancy advantage for the untutored boys was over two points.)

The results described were based on post-testing only two months after the initiation of the experiment. Follow-up testing was undertaken seven months after the end of the basic experiment. In reasoning IQ, the boys who had been both tutored and expected to bloom intellectually made up the expectancy disadvantage they had shown after just two months. Now, their performance change was just like that of the control group children, both groups showing an IQ loss of four points over the nine-month period. Compared to these boys who had been given both or neither of the two experimental treatments, the boys who had been given either tutoring or the benefit of favorable expectations showed significantly greater gains in reasoning IQ scores. Relative to the control group children, those who were tutored showed a 10-point advantage while those who were expected to bloom showed a 12-point advantage.

While both tutoring and a favorable teacher expectation were effective in raising relative IQ scores, it appeared that when these two treatments were applied simultaneously, they were ineffective in producing IQ gains over the period from the beginning of the experiment to the nine-month follow-up. One possible explanation of this finding is that the presence of both treatments simultaneously led the boys to perceive too much pressure. The same pattern of results reported for reasoning IQ was also obtained when verbal IQ and total IQ were considered, though the interaction was significant only in the case of total IQ.

In the experiment under discussion, a number of other measures of the boys' behavior were available as were observations of the day-camp counselors' behavior toward the boys. Preliminary analysis suggests that boys who had been expected to bloom intellectually were given less attention by the counselors and developed a greater degree of independence compared to the boys of the control group.

Another study, this time conducted in an East Coast school with upper-middle class pupils, again showed the largest effect of teachers' expectancies to occur when the measure was of reasoning IQ (Conn, Edwards, Rosenthal, and Crowne, 1968). In this study, both the boys and girls who were expected to bloom intellectually showed greater gains in reasoning IQ than did the boys and girls of the control group and the magnitude of the expectancy effect favored the girls very slightly. Also in this study, we had available a measure of the children's accuracy in judging the vocal expressions of emotion of adult speakers. It was of considerable theoretical interest to find that greater benefits of favorable teacher expectations accrued to those children who were more accurate in judging the emotional tone expressed in an adult female's voice. These findings, taken together with the research of Adair and Epstein (1968) and others (Rosenthal, 1969) described earlier, give a strong suggestion that vocal cues may be important in the covert communication of interpersonal expectations in both teachers and psychological experimenters.

In all the experiments described so far, the same IQ measure was employed, the Flanagan (1960) Tests of General Ability. Also employing the same instrument, Claiborn (1968) found among first graders a tendency for children he designated as potential bloomers to gain less in IQ than the children of the control group (two-tail $p < .15$). A similar tendency was obtained by Rosenthal and Anderson (1969) employing somewhat older children (two-tail $p < .17$).

With fifth-grade boys as his subjects and males as teachers, Pitt (1956) found no effect on achievement scores of arbitrarily adding or subtracting 10 IQ points on the children's records. In her study, Heiserman (1967) found no effect of teacher expectations on her seventh graders' stated levels of occupational aspiration.

There have been two studies in which teachers' expectations were varied not for specific children within a classroom but rather for classrooms as a whole (Biegen, 1968; Flowers, 1966). In both cases, the performance gains were greater for those classrooms expected by their teachers to show the better performance.

A radically different type of performance measure was employed in the research by Burnham (1968): not intelligence or scholastic achievement this time, but swimming ability. His subjects were boys and girls aged 7-14 attending a summer camp for the disadvantaged. None of the children could swim at the beginning of the two-week experimental period. Half the children were alleged to the camp staff to have shown unusual potential for learning to swim as judged from a battery of psychological tests. Children were, of course, assigned to the "high potential" group at random. At the end of the two-week period of the experiment, all the children were retested on the standard Red Cross Beginner Swimmer Test. Those children who had been expected to show greater improvement in swimming ability showed greater improvement than did the children of the control group.

In their experiment, Meichenbaum, Bowers, and Ross (1968) also employed a very different type of criterion variable: appropriateness of classroom behavior. The choice of this variable was itself particularly appropriate, in view of the fact that these workers employed as their research population a sample of institutionalized adolescent female offenders. Two weeks before the beginning of this experiment, classroom observers, who knew nothing of the experimental manipulations to come, began to record the behavior of both the girls and their teachers. These observations continued through the entire experiment which, remarkably enough, lasted only two weeks. Within two weeks after teachers were given the names of the "potential bloomers," the designated children already showed a significantly greater improvement in classroom behavior than did the children of the control group. This experiment was particularly important in suggesting that the benefits of favorable teacher expectations were associated with an increase in the teachers' positively toned attention to the designated children.

We may conclude now with the brief description of just one more experiment, this one conducted by W. Victor Beez (1968), who kindly made his data available for the analyses to follow. This time the pupils were 60 preschoolers from a summer Head Start program. Each child was taught the meaning of a series of symbols by one teacher. Half the 60 teachers had been led to expect good symbol-learning and half had been led to expect poor symbol-learning. Most (77 percent) of the children alleged to have better intellectual prospects learned five or more symbols, but only 13 percent of the children alleged to have poorer intellectual prospects learned five or more symbols. In this study the children's actual performance was assessed by an experimenter who did not know what the child's teacher had been told about the child's intellectual prospects. Teachers who had been given favorable expectations about their pupil tried to teach more symbols to their pupil than did the teachers given unfavorable expectations about their pupil. The difference in teaching effort was dramatic. Eight or more symbols were taught by 87 percent of the teachers expecting better performance, but only 13 percent of the teachers expecting poorer performance tried to teach that many symbols to their pupil.

These results suggest that a teacher's expectation about a pupil's performance may sometimes be translated not into subtle vocal nuances or general increases in positively toned attention, but rather into overt and even dramatic alterations in teaching style. The magnitude of the effect of teacher expectations found by Beez is also worthy of comment. In all the earlier studies described, one group of children had been singled out for favorable expectations while nothing was said of the remaining children of the control group. In Beez' short-term experiment it seemed more justified to give negative as well as positive expectations about some of the children. Perhaps the very large effects of teacher expectancy obtained by Beez were due to the creation of strong equal but opposite expectations in the minds of the different teachers. Since strong negative expectations doubtless exist in the real world of classrooms, Beez' procedure may give the better estimate of the effects of teacher expectations as they occur in everyday life.

In the experiment by Beez it seems clear that the dramatic differences in teaching style accounted at least in part for the dramatic differences in pupil learning. However, not all of the obtained differences in learners' learning were due to the differences in teachers' teaching. Within each condition of teacher expectation, for example, there was no relationship between number of symbols taught and number of symbols learned. In addition, it was also possible to compare the performances of just those children of the two conditions who had been given an exactly equal amount of teaching benefit. Even holding teaching benefits constant, the difference favored significantly the children believed to be superior though the magnitude of the effect was now diminished by nearly half.

We have now seen at least a brief description of 13 studies of the effects of interpersonal expectancies in natural learning situations. That is too many to hold easily in mind and Table 3 provides a convenient summary. (For each experiment the directional standard normal deviate [z] associated with each p level is given,

Study	Results p	z	Criterion
1. Anderson and Rosenthal, 1968	—	0.00 [a]	Total IQ
2. Beez, 1968	.000002	+4.67	Symbol learning
3. Biegen, 1968	.002	+2.89 [b]	Achievement
4. Burnham, 1968; Burnham and Hartsough, 1968	.005	+2.61 [a]	Swimming score
5. Claiborn, 1968	(−).08	−1.45 [a]	Total IQ
6. Conn, Edwards, Rosenthal, and Crowne, 1968	—	0.00 [a]	Total IQ
7. Flowers, 1966	.06	+1.60	Achievement + IQ
8. Heiserman, 1967	—	0.00	Aspiration
9. Meichenbaum, Bowers, and Ross, 1968	.02	+2.02 [b]	Classroom behavior
10. Pitt, 1956	—	0.00	Achievement
11. Rosenthal and Anderson, 1969	(−).08	−1.40 [b]	Total IQ
12. Rosenthal and Evans, 1968	—	0.00 [a,b]	Total IQ
13. Rosenthal and Jacobson, 1968	.02	+2.11 [a]	Total IQ
Overall	.0002	+3.61	

[a] Indicates the interaction of teacher expectancy and some other variable.
[b] Preliminary data.

Table 3. Teacher Expectancy Effects in 13 Experiments

as well as a brief identification of the dependent variables employed. As was the custom in an earlier paper [Rosenthal, 1969], a standard normal deviate greater than −1.28 and smaller than +1.28 has been recorded as zero.) Of the five experiments tabulated as showing no main effect of teacher expectation, it should be noted that at least three of them showed significant interactions of teacher expectation with some other primary variable such as special tutoring (Study 1), accuracy of emotion perception (6), and sex of pupil (12). The combined one-tail p of the main effects of teacher expectancy in the studies shown in Table 3 is less than 1 in 5,000. It would take an additional 50 studies of a mean associated z value of 0.00 to bring the overall combined p to above .05.

Shall we view this set of experiments in natural learning situations in isolation or would it be wiser to see them simply as more of the same type of experiment that has been discussed throughout this paper? Since the type of experimental manipulation involved in the laboratory studies is essentially the same as that employed in the studies beyond the laboratory, it seems more parsimonious to view all the studies as members of the same set. If, in addition to the communality of experimental procedures, we find it plausible to conclude a communality of outcome patterns between the laboratory and field experiments, perhaps we can have the greater convenience and power of speaking of just one type of effect of interpersonal expectancy. Table 4 allows each reader to make his own judgment or test for "goodness of fit." At each level of p we find the proportion of laboratory and educational studies reaching that or a lower level of p. The agreement between the two types of studies appears to be remarkably close.

If there were a systematic difference in sample size between studies conducted in laboratories and those involving teachers, then we might expect to find that for similar z's or p's the average effects would be smaller in magnitude for the set comprised of larger sample sizes. For this reason it seems necessary also to compare magnitudes of expectancy effect for studies involving experimenters and teachers. Table 5 shows this comparison. For 59 studies of experimenters and for seven studies of teachers, it was possible to

p (one-tail)	Experimenters	Teachers	Total
$< .10$	48%	46%	47%
$< .05$	34%	38%	34%
$< .01$	17%	23%	17%
$< .001$	12%	8%	11%
$< .0001$	5%	8%	5%
Grand sum z	+100.86	+13.05	+113.91
$\sqrt{\text{Number of Experiments}}$	$\sqrt{103}$	$\sqrt{13}$	$\sqrt{116}$
Combined z	+ 9.94	+ 3.61	+ 10.58

Table 4. Percentage of Studies of Expectancy Effect Obtaining Results at Various p Levels Among Experimenters and Teachers

	Experimenters	Teachers	Total
Number of Studies Included	59	7	66
Percentage of These Studies with $p < .10$ (one-tail)	49%	43%	48%
Number of Experimenters or Teachers	548	140	688
Mean Number per Study	9	20	10
Percentage of Biased Experimenters or Teachers	70%	67%	70%

Table 5. Percentage of Experimenters and Teachers Showing Expectancy Effects

calculate the proportion of each that was affected in the predicted direction by their expectancy. Again the agreement is very good. About 7 out of 10 experimenters or teachers can be expected to show the effects of their expectation on the performance of their subjects or pupils.

This paper began its discussion of interpersonal expectancy effects by suggesting that the expectancy of the behavioral researcher might function as a self-fulfilling prophecy. This unintended effect of the research hypothesis itself must be regarded as a potentially damaging artifact. But interpersonal self-fulfilling prophecies do not operate only in laboratories and while, when there, they may act as artifacts, they are more than that. Interpersonal expectancy effects occur also among teachers and, there seems no reason to doubt, among others as well. What started life as an artifact continues as an interpersonal variable of theoretical and practical importance.

Some Implications

The implications of the research described in this paper are of several kinds. There are methodological implications for the conduct of educational research, and these have been discussed elsewhere in detail (Rosenthal, 1966; Rosenthal and Jacobson, 1968). There are implications for the further investigation of unintentional influence processes, especially when these processes result in interpersonal self-fulfilling prophecies; and some of these have been discussed. Finally, there are some possible implications for the educational enterprise; and some of these will be suggested briefly.

Over time, our educational policy question has changed from "who ought to be educated" to "who is capable of being educated." The ethical question has been traded in for the scientific question. For those children whose educability is in doubt there is a label. They are the educationally, or culturally, or socioeconomically deprived children and, as things stand now, they appear not to be able to learn as do those who are more advantaged. The advantaged and the disadvantaged differ in parental income, in parental values, in scores on various tests of achievement and ability, and often in skin color and other phenotypic expressions of genetic heritage. Quite inseparable from these differences between the advantaged and the disadvantaged are the differences in their teachers' expectations for what they can achieve in school. There are no experiments to show that a change in pupils' skin color will lead to improved intellectual performance. There are, however, the experiments described in this paper to show that change in teacher expectation can lead to improved intellectual performance and related behaviors.

In none of the relevant experiments was anything done directly for the "disadvantaged" child. There were no crash programs to improve his school achievement, no trips to museums or art galleries. There was only the belief that the children bore watching, that they had intellectual competencies that would in due course be revealed. What was done in these programs of educational change was done directly for teachers, only indirectly for their pupils.

Perhaps, then, it is the teacher to whom we should direct more of our research attention. If we could learn how he is able to effect dramatic improvement in his pupils' competence without formal changes in his teaching methods, then we could teach other teachers to do the same. If further research shows that it is possible to select teachers whose untrained interactional style does for most of his pupils what teachers did for the allegedly special children described in this paper, it may be possible to combine sophisticated teacher selection and placement with teacher training to optimize the learning of all pupils.

As teacher training institutions begin to teach the possibility that teachers' expectations of their pupils' performance may serve as self-fulfilling prophecies, there may be a new expectancy created. The new expectancy may be that children can learn more than had been believed possible, an expectation held by many educational theorists, though for quite different reasons (for example, Bruner, 1960; Skinner, 1968). The new expectancy, at the very least, will make it more difficult, when they encounter the educationally disadvantaged, for teachers to shrug and say or think, "Well, after all, what can you expect?"

As Lenore Jacobson (Rosenthal and Jacobson, 1968) has said:

> The man on the street may be permitted his opinions and prophecies of the unkempt children loitering in a dreary schoolyard. The teacher in the schoolroom may need to learn that those same prophecies within her may be fulfilled; she is no casual passer-by. Perhaps Pygmalion in the classroom is more her role.[2]

---

[2] Robert Rosenthal and Lenore Jacobson. *Pygmalion in the Classroom: Teacher Expectation and Pupils' Intellectual Development.* New York: Holt, Rinehart and Winston, Inc., 1968.

References

J. G. Adair and J. S. Epstein. "Verbal Cues in the Mediation of Experimenter Bias." *Psychological Reports* 22: 1045-53; 1968.

G. W. Allport. "The Role of Expectancy." In: H. Cantril, editor. *Tensions That Cause Wars.* Urbana, Illinois: University of Illinois Press, 1950. pp. 43-78.

D. F. Anderson and R. Rosenthal. "Some Effects of Interpersonal Expectancy and Social Interaction on Institutionalized Retarded Children." *Proceedings of the 76th Annual Convention of the American Psychological Association,* 1968. pp. 479-80.

W. V. Beez. "Influence of Biased Psychological Reports on Teacher Behavior and Pupil Performance." *Proceedings of the 76th Annual Convention of the American Psychological Association,* 1968. pp. 605-606.

D. A. Biegen. Unpublished data, University of Cincinnati, 1968.

J. S. Bruner. *The Process of Education.* Cambridge, Massachusetts: Harvard University Press, 1960.

J. R. Burnham. "Experimenter Bias and Lesion Labeling." Unpublished manuscript, Purdue University, 1966.

J. R. Burnham. "Effects of Experimenter's Expectancies on Children's Ability To Learn To Swim." Unpublished master's thesis, Purdue University, 1968.

J. R. Burnham and D. M. Hartsough. "Effect of Experimenter's Expectancies ('The Rosenthal Effect') on Children's Ability To Learn To Swim." Paper presented at the meeting of the Midwestern Psychological Association, Chicago, May 1968.

W. L. Claiborn. "An Investigation of the Relationship Between Teacher Expectancy, Teacher Behavior, and Pupil Performance." Unpublished doctoral dissertation, Syracuse University, 1968.

K. B. Clark. "Educational Stimulation of Racially Disadvantaged Children." In: A. H. Passow, editor. *Education in Depressed Areas.* New York: Bureau of Publications, Teachers College, Columbia University, 1963. pp. 142-62.

L. K. Conn, C. N. Edwards, A. Rosenthal, and D. Crowne. "Perception of Emotion and Response to Teachers' Expectancy by Elementary School Children." *Psychological Reports* 22: 27-34; 1968.

J. Cooper, L. Eisenberg, J. Roberts, and B. S. Dohrenwend. "The Effect of Experimenter Expectancy and Preparatory Effort on Belief in the Probable Occurrence of Future Events." *Journal of Social Psychology* 71: 221-26; 1967.

J. C. Flanagan. *Test of General Ability: Technical Report.* Chicago: Science Research Associates, 1960.

C. E. Flowers. "Effects of an Arbitrary Accelerated Group Placement on the Tested Academic Achievement of Educationally Disadvantaged Students." Unpublished doctoral dissertation, Teachers College, Columbia University, 1966.

M. S. Heiserman. "The Relationship Between Teacher Expectations and Pupil Occupational Aspirations." Unpublished master's thesis, Iowa State University, Ames, 1967.

R. W. Johnson. "Subject Performance as Affected by Experimenter Expectancy, Sex of Experimenter, and Verbal Reinforcement." Unpublished master's thesis, University of New Brunswick, 1967.

L. L. Larrabee and L. D. Kleinsasser. "The Effect of Experimenter Bias on WISC Performance." Unpublished manuscript, Psychological Associates, St. Louis, 1967.

S. J. Marwit. "An Investigation of the Communication of Tester-Bias by Means of Modeling." Unpublished doctoral dissertation, State University of New York at Buffalo, 1968.

D. H. Meichenbaum, K. S. Bowers, and R. R. Ross. "A Behavioral Analysis of Teacher Expectancy Effect." Unpublished manuscript, University of Waterloo, Ontario, Canada, 1968.

R. K. Merton. "The Self-Fulfilling Prophecy." *Antioch Review* 8: 193-210; 1968.

O. Pfungst. *Clever Hans (The Horse of Mr. von Osten): A Contribution to Experimental, Animal, and Human Psychology.* Translated by C. L. Rahn. New York: Holt, 1911. Republished by Holt, Rinehart and Winston, Inc., 1965.

C. C. V. Pitt. "An Experimental Study of the Effects of Teachers' Knowledge or Incorrect Knowledge of Pupil IQ's on Teachers' Attitudes and Practices and Pupils' Attitudes and Achievement." Unpublished doctoral dissertation, Columbia University, 1956.

A. M. Raffetto. "Experimenter Effects on Subjects' Reported Hallucinatory Experiences Under Visual and Auditory Deprivation." Paper presented at the meeting of the Midwestern Psychological Association, Chicago, May 1968.

R. Rosenthal. "The Effect of the Experimenter on the Results of Psychological Research." In: B. A. Maher, editor. *Progress in Experimental Personality Research.* Vol. 1. New York: Academic Press, 1964. pp. 79-114. (a)

R. Rosenthal. "Experimenter Outcome-Orientation and the Results of the Psychological Experiment." *Psychological Bulletin* 61: 405-12; 1964. (b)

R. Rosenthal. "Clever Hans: A Case Study of Scientific Method." Introduction to O. Pfungst. *Clever Hans: (The Horse of Mr. von Osten).* New York: Holt, Rinehart and Winston, Inc., 1965. pp. ix-xlii.

R. Rosenthal. *Experimenter Effects in Behavioral Research.* New York: Appleton-Century-Crofts, 1966.

R. Rosenthal. "Interpersonal Expectations: Effects of the Experimenter's Hypothesis." In: R. Rosenthal and R. L. Rosnow, editors. *Artifact in Behavioral Research.* New York: Academic Press, Inc., 1969. pp. 181-277.

R. Rosenthal and D. F. Anderson. "Teacher Behavior and the Mediation of Teacher Expectancy Effects." Unpublished data, Harvard University, 1969.

R. Rosenthal and J. Evans. Unpublished data, Harvard University, 1968.

R. Rosenthal and K. L. Fode. "The Effect of Experimenter Bias on the Performance of the Albino Rat." *Behavioral Science* 8: 183-89; 1963. (a)

R. Rosenthal and K. L. Fode. "Three Experiments in Experimenter Bias." *Psychological Reports* 12: 491-511; 1963. (b)

R. Rosenthal and L. Jacobson. *Pygmalion in the Classroom: Teacher Expectation and Pupils' Intellectual Development.* New York: Holt, Rinehart and Winston, Inc., 1968.

B. F. Skinner. "Teaching Science in High School—What Is Wrong?" *Science* 159: 704-10; 1968.

E. J. Zoble. "Interaction of Subject and Experimenter Expectancy Effects in a Tone Length Discrimination Task." Unpublished A.B. thesis, Franklin and Marshall College, Lancaster, Pennsylvania, 1968.

Appendix A
Experimenter Expectancy Effects Obtained in 33 Laboratories

Investigator [a]	Location	Number of Studies	Overall z [b]	Percentage of Studies with $p \leqslant .10$ (one-tail)
1. Adair	Manitoba	6	+ 2.04 [c]	50%
2. Adler	Wellesley	3	0.00	33%
3. Barber	Medfield [d]	5	0.00 [c]	00%
4. Becker	Saskatchewan	3	0.00	00%
5. Bootzin	Purdue	3	0.00 [c]	67%
6. Burnham	Earlham	1	+ 1.95	100%
7. Carlson	Hamline	2	0.00 [c]	00%
8. Cooper	C C, CUNY	1	+ 3.37	100%
9. Getter	Connecticut	1	0.00	00%
10. Harrington	Iowa State	2	+ 2.54	100%
11. Hartry	Occidental	2	+ 6.15	100%
12. Horn	George Washington	1	+ 2.01	100%
13. Ison	Rochester	2	+ 5.11	100%
14. Johnson	New Brunswick	1	+ 3.89 [c]	100%
15. Kennedy	Tennessee	2	+ 1.61 [c]	50%
16. Larrabee	South Dakota	1	+ 1.60	100%
17. Marcia	SUNY, Buffalo	2	+ 3.58	100%
18. Masling	SUNY, Buffalo	2	+ 1.45 [c]	50%
19. McFall	Ohio State	2	0.00 [c]	00%
20. Minor	Chicago	4	0.00 [c]	25%
21. Moffat	British Columbia	1	0.00	00%
22. Peel	Memphis State	1	+ 3.58	100%
23. Persinger	Fergus Falls [d]	2	+ 2.50 [c]	100%
24. Raffetto	San Francisco State	1	+ 5.24 [c]	100%
25. Rosenthal	Harvard	35	+ 4.83 [c]	49%
26. Silverman	SUNY, Buffalo	1	+ 1.88 [c]	100%
27. Timaeus	Cologne	3	0.00 [c]	33%
28. Uno	Keio (Tokyo)	5	− 1.86 [c]	00%
29. Wartenberg-Ekren	Marquette	1	0.00	00%

Appendix A (continued)

Investigator [a]	Location	Number of Studies	Overall z [b]	Percentage of Studies with $p \leq .10$ (one-tail)
30. Weick	Purdue	1	+ 2.33	100%
31. Wessler	St. Louis	3	0.00 [c]	33%
32. Zegers	Illinois	1	0.00	00%
33. Zoble	Franklin & Marshall	2	+ 4.06	100%
	Total	(103)	+57.86	
	Combined z	—	+10.08	(p infinitely small)
	Mean p		.040	
	Median p		.054	

[a] For references to specific experiments see Rosenthal (1969).

[b] Standard normal deviate associated with overall p per laboratory.

[c] Indicates that experimenter expectancy interacted with other variables at $z \geq /1.28/$.

[d] Indicates a state hospital. All other locations are colleges or universities.

Schooling and Authority: Comments on the Unstudied Curriculum

ROBERT DREEBEN

MUCH of what we know about human development derives from a large body of research inspired by the idea that the task of adults is to civilize invading barbarians—young children, that is. Freud has described their barbarities in some detail. It used to be said that life begins at 40. Now we are advised not to trust anyone over 30; and we contemplate these changing conceptions of the ages of man with the knowledge, deep in our minds, that we are all washed up at six. So much for caricature. I prefer to believe that psychological changes—important ones and of varying kinds—occur during all phases of the life span,[1] that the course of development includes not only the socialization [2] of

---

[1] See, for example: Leonard D. Cain. "Life Course and Social Structure." In: Robert E. L. Faris, editor. *Handbook of Modern Sociology.* Chicago: Rand McNally & Company, 1964. pp. 272-309; and Orville G. Brim. "Adult Socialization." In: John A. Clausen, editor. *Socialization and Society.* Boston: Little, Brown and Company, 1968. pp. 183-226.

[2] For a more complete exposition of this argument, see: Alex Inkeles. "Social Structure and the Socialization of Competence." *Harvard Educational Review* 36 (3): 265-83; 1966. According to Inkeles, "Research on socialization addresses itself predominantly to understanding how the child learns to manage his own body and his primary needs. It inquires mainly how the child is guided in learning to manage the intake of food, the discharge of waste, and the control of sexual and aggressive impulses. . . . [Little] is done in socialization research to study the acquisition of a broad array of qualities, skills, habits, and motives which are essential to the adequate social functioning of any [adult] man or woman. . . ." (p. 266). "I approach competence mainly as a requirement for participation in contemporary and 'modern' urban industrial settings." (pp. 267-68).

childhood impulses but learning the varied requirements of adult life, and should be formulated in terms of those requirements.

Specifically, I am concerned here with the relevance of schooling to the development of capacities that enable people to participate in relationships of authority as adults. This is a question of many parts, only some of which can be covered in a short paper; but at the minimum, some description of the nature of schooling and of authority is required as well as a formulation of how they are related. To scotch any misunderstanding at the outset: my argument will be theoretical and speculative, largely uncontaminated by factual information.

Observations About Schooling

Three initial considerations color my treatment of schooling. First, I am concerned almost exclusively with the organizational properties of schools, not with curriculum or with methods of instruction. Schools are social settings with a peculiar set of attributes; and I contend that part of their impact can be attributed to children's experiences in dealing with the demands and opportunities that the setting itself provides (which is not to say that they learn nothing from instruction).

Second, children enter school after an extended period as dependent members of a family, a small social unit usually characterized by strong emotional bonds among its members, and in other ways very different from school classrooms. One of these differences is that authority relations between parents and children, unlike those between teachers and pupils, are based largely on long-standing bonds of personal attachment and affection. Yet, children maintain their connections with the family after entering school; and this suggests that the school's contribution adds to, but does not replace, what is learned at home.

Third, schooling is not a unitary process from beginning to end. It is divided into stages, or levels, with each level an organizational entity characterized by distinct structural properties (in addition to obvious similarities). Each level provides experiences related to these organizational differences but unlike those preceding it.

Observations About Authority

Authority is a complex idea usually associated with subordination and superordination, hierarchy, and the giving and taking of orders. This description, however, is too general because it encompasses all types of authority relations, and I am concerned with how children gain the capacities to participate in *different* kinds of relationships. If father-child authority relationships are prototypical, as some maintain, that does not mean they are identical with all others; consequently, we need to discover how children acquire the skills necessary to participate in the *variety* of these relationships that adult life entails.

Most studies of authority treat it primarily within family and large bureaucratic settings, in both of which the hierarchy is fairly clear. But by shifting perspective from the setting to the person, one finds that adults are involved in a vast array of situations where considerations of authority arise: in their capacities as parents, students, supervisors, executives, professionals, employees, parishioners, customers, patients, passengers, and the like. Note that this list refers to people both in superior *and* subordinate positions, and to situations in which the basis of authority varies: by generation, expertise, power, contract, and the like. Most important for the task of schooling is that modern adult life requires each person to participate across a wide range of situations more or less competently, and that something has to change in people so that they can deal with more than just the familial forms of authority. There is reason to suspect that schooling contributes to this change.

Ideological Considerations

Americans traditionally feel uneasy about authority and about its rhetoric. People connected with the public schools have felt so more intensely than others and to a degree that they fashion a euphemistic language to avoid talking about authority. Perhaps this is symptomatic of social reality conflicting with ideological egalitarianism. But asking how the American public educational system contributes to the working of the economic and political systems, in the area of authority, does not allow the luxury of adhering to ideological myths. Before proceeding, then, I wish to question two of them.

The first assumes an incompatibility between authority and democracy; it is typically expressed in statements such as this: "To create a democratic citizenry, the schools themselves must be organized democratically." Shibboleths like this one ignore some of the defining characteristics of democratic polities: periodic or regular turnover in office by election, a widely enfranchised citizen-electorate, a separation of at least executive and judicial functions, majority rule for the election of candidates (but not necessarily on policy matters), and voluntary participation. None of these conditions obtains in schools or in classrooms primarily because schools are designed for the performance of technical tasks, not for the mobilization of a populace to support a government; accordingly, one finds school positions filled by appointment according to criteria of expertise, with persons (teachers) empowered both to make policy and to judge—an arrangement scarcely consistent with an enfranchised pupil electorate.

The democratic ideologues in the educational community have simply fastened on the one idea of participation by subordinates—conscripted subordinates at that—and have confused that fragment with the whole. The result at best has been greater sensitivity to the interests of pupils (though this on occasion has been taken to extremes) and some ritual motions toward student government; but this should not be confused with democracy. The important questions remain open: given the characteristics of the democratic polity in America, what capacities and states of mind—particularly those pertaining to authority—are consistent with participation in it? And what contribution does the school make to their acquisition?

The second concerns the idea of authoritarianism. The recent emergence of Anglo-Saxon invective in public discourse has shunted some of the older forms of verbal assault aside; but it was not long ago that the worst thing you could call someone, at least in some circles, was an authoritarian personality. In schools, authoritarianism is usually construed as one style of teaching (a bad one) and contrasted with the democratic (or good) style. Part of the problem in this comparison arises from the images that the term "authoritarian" conjures up: autocracy, discipline, arbitrariness, and authority itself, a perfectly appropriate word whose meaning became sullied through guilt by word association. In this particular case, the loss of a good word because of its unsavory ideological aroma has contributed to the failure to ask potentially fruitful questions; for as long as there is an educational preoccupation with creating democratic teachers (whatever that means), there will be little impetus to inquire into the nature of prevailing authority relations in classrooms and schools and into their contribution to shaping capacities relevant to authority situations in adult life.

The most obvious evidence that authority relationships are part of classroom life is that teachers assume final responsibility for directing activities: they plan the work, make assignments, judge the products, keep order, reward and punish. (None of this denies that pupils assume some of these responsibilities in many classrooms, but where they do, it is by the teacher's leave; teachers delegate certain responsibilities to pupils but not their authority.) This "evidence" is really a complex set of problems masquerading as a simple and familiar observation, and I wish to turn to the problems and the circumstances surrounding them.

School Characteristics and the Exercise of Authority

First, unlike a parent, a teacher occupies an organizational position gained by acquiring credentials and assigned mainly according to criteria of competence and appropriateness, not by personal or filial association. Second, the teacher has charge of a collective enterprise comprising each pupil individually and all pupils in the aggregate. Third, like it or not, both teacher and pupils are assigned to each other by a combination of chance and administrative convenience, and typically remain together for somewhat less than a year; that is, a classroom is the site of an involuntary association of pupils and their teacher for a substantial period of time. Fourth, classrooms possess a public quality in which the words and deeds of everyone are highly, though not completely, visible.[3]

Good Will

Because their conventional meanings and connotations are so different, it is strange to juxtapose the terms "authority" and "good will"; but the situation of young children just entering school requires just that. The reason, I maintain, is that the teacher's first task is to get children to like school. Some children, of course, are favorably disposed before they enter, others not; but even those who begin gladly are not necessarily aware that the experiences awaiting them will be very different from what they are used to at home, perhaps even frightening and alien. They will get less attention, affection, and individual indulgence; they will be expected to do what everybody else does at the same time—do their work, sit still, keep quiet, line up, pay attention—whether or not they feel like it.

[3] Each of these statements has qualifications too familiar to enumerate; but on the whole, they summarize the prevailing situation far more than they summarize its exceptions.

And the judgment of their work and conduct rapidly becomes public knowledge despite teachers' efforts to judge privately, a fact of school life that may be particularly threatening to the self-esteem of those who do poorly.[4]

Since a teacher is unlikely to know in advance which pupils will find school pleasurable, painful, or something in between, one strategy is to develop among them all a sense of diffuse attachment to the school and to her personally. This is what I mean by the creation of good will: a teacher's attempts to make the first encounters gratuitously pleasurable, to express kindness, sympathy, and respect, without a *quid pro quo*. These initial experiences are important because children will realize before long that the teacher and other adult members of the school community make demands and enforce rules that they must manage without customary supports of family and friends.

To state the issue more technically, the teacher must begin to establish a basis of legitimacy for the school regime, one that operates on different principles from the family. One of the primary differences in the two regimes concerns the exercise of authority—hence the ostensibly odd connection between good will and authority. For the expression of good will in the earliest grades becomes one mechanism for children to make the transition from one regime to another with their distinct premises for conduct. Unfortunately, we know exceedingly little about how good will is created, or how many teachers consciously create it as a strategy, but that it is a problem in authority is unmistakable, and particularly for the child who discovers that if he follows the rules of the school regime he consistently ends up at the bottom of the heap and pays the personal price of confronting public recognition of his own inadequacy. Why should such a child, the chronic loser, accept schooling as right and just?[5]

Although creating good will is one means of establishing the legitimacy of the school regime, it has additional importance for building a sense of solidarity between pupils and their teacher within a classroom, since initially the teacher's relationship to pupils is neither familiar nor familial. There is no reason to assume that,

[4] Of course, where home life is squalid and neglectful, school may provide welcome relief from a bad situation.

[5] For a more complete discussion of the legitimacy problem in schools, see: Talcott Parsons. "The School Class as a Social System: Some of Its Functions in American Society." *Harvard Educational Review* 29 (4): 304-13; 1959.

because children implicitly acknowledge the legitimacy of parental authority, they automatically generalize that legitimacy to all adults, especially under non-familial circumstances.

Sanctions

Particularly in the earliest grades, where problems of separating children from their families can be acute, the teacher must acquire those personal resources most necessary to become the official sanctioning and order-giving agent in the classroom. Teachers judge pupils' work (and judge them as persons as well) in a variety of ways, but the coin of the realm in school is grades. No matter how clinical, euphemistic, evasive, or noncompetitive the format of a report card, it is a dull child (or parent) who cannot rapidly translate it into evaluative A's, B's, and C's.

But why should these otherwise neutral symbols take on the quality of sanctions? Why should pupils—at least substantial numbers of them—accept these marks as assessments of their work and ascribe enough importance to them that good marks elicit gratification and poor ones displeasure and even at times produce an inducement to improve? And furthermore, how do these events come about? I do not pretend to know the answers to these questions, but there is ample reason to believe that teachers cannot take the sanctioning properties of grades for granted, and that they must do something to infuse innocuous symbols with power sufficient to influence the conduct of some if not most pupils; for unless pupils acknowledge that grades make a difference in the way teachers intend them to, the teacher's position and power as a judge become weak.[6]

Although the mechanisms by which this happens (and in some cases fails to happen) remain obscure, the important thing is that the early years of school represent the first situation in which children are judged *systematically* according to abstract standards of performance. The teacher certainly administers the sanctions, and most probably the personal relationship he establishes with his pupils contributes to the acceptance or rejection of the standards (in ways we do not yet understand), but the classroom in this respect resembles judgmental situations more typical of non-familial adult life than it does life in the family. This is not to deny that parents judge the performance of their children; they do, but not in a way

[6] I use grades here only as an example—though an important one—with full knowledge that teachers have other sanctions at their disposal.

that clarifies the distinction between the person judging and the abstract standard for judgment. The crucial difference in the child's experience is that in school the principle for judging performance applies across the board to an aggregation of age peers, while in the family, where children differ in age-related capacities, principles of judgment vary with their ages. Under these circumstances, it is difficult for a child to tell whether judgment is a personal matter between parents and each particular child or whether the personal and impersonal elements are actually distinct.[7]

Whatever rhetoric teachers use to describe relationships of authority—meeting the needs of children, making the work so interesting that discipline problems never arise, creating a democratic climate, and so on through the list of related fantasies—they must still exact at least minimum compliance so that pupils get their work done and conduct themselves civilly both in the classroom and in the school at large. This is the exercise of authority in the conventional sense: getting others to do voluntarily what is expected of them.

Note, however, what this formulation takes for granted: that subordinates *already* acknowledge (even if implicitly) the superior's right to give orders and the principles of legitimacy underlying them, that there is agreement about the areas of conduct over which authority can be exercised, that both parties recognize a disobedient act and acknowledge the superior's right to sanction it.

In effect, ongoing relationships of authority presume that the rules of the game governing them have been settled.[8] The earliest phases of schooling are substantially concerned with the settlement of these rules, but once they are settled, teachers become more involved with the exercise of authority than with its creation.

---

[7] For a more complete discussion of the problems of judgment within families and classrooms, see: Robert Dreeben. *On What Is Learned in School.* Reading, Massachusetts: Addison-Wesley Publishing Company, Inc., 1968. Chapters 2 and 3, pp. 74-84.

[8] For discussions of established relationships of authority, see: Max Weber. *The Theory of Social and Economic Organization.* Translated by A. M. Henderson and Talcott Parsons. Glencoe, Illinois: The Free Press, Inc., 1947. pp. 324-63; Peter M. Blau. *The Dynamics of Bureaucracy.* Revised edition. Chicago: University of Chicago Press, 1963. pp. 207-28; Alvin W. Gouldner. *Patterns of Industrial Bureaucracy.* Glencoe, Illinois: The Free Press, Inc., 1954. pp. 157-206; and Amitai Etzioni. *A Comparative Analysis of Complex Organizations.* New York: The Free Press of Glencoe, Inc., 1961. pp. 3-67.

Implications of the Milieu

Simply stated, the teacher's tasks in exercising authority are to assign work, see that it is done, judge it, oversee classroom activities, encourage desirable conduct, and punish infractions; whether the desired outcomes occur is problematic. Yet the formulation, though plausible, is incomplete because it omits all reference to the social context of the classroom. For example: (a) because classrooms are collective and public, a teacher must control and prescribe work for many children at once; (b) since teachers sustain contact with pupils for much of each day and for the better part of a year, the exercise of authority must be adapted to those time conditions rather than to the situation at the moment with little regard for long-run implications; (c) schools differ by level: elementary teachers are predominantly women responsible for teaching nearly all subjects to the same group of about 30 pupils, while secondary teachers (consisting of about equal numbers of men and women) are departmentalized according to subject matter and meet successive aggregates of different pupils during the day.

Although these school characteristics are familiar, some of their implications for exercising authority are not. First, since classrooms are collective entities in their own right *and also* contain individuals with unique characteristics (save age, which is relatively constant), teachers, in assigning work with the intention that pupils will do it, must adapt their demands to accommodate the full range of capacities that pupils bring with them. At the same time, they must act without prejudice for or against by treating and judging all pupils by the same standards. Obviously, these two injunctions create a dilemma for gaining compliance. If the range of capacities is wide, applying the same standards to everyone in the interest of fairness will make some members of a class unhappy, bored, frustrated, or resentful; similarly, treating some pupils as special cases—the highly talented, the poor achievers, the solid citizens in the middle—can violate the principle of equity and open the teacher to charges of favoritism. The strategies for dealing with the dilemma are well-known: impaling oneself on one of its horns, aiming for the middle while losing the rest, stratifying the class by ability and reaping the anxieties of pupils and parents that the ensuing status distinction produces.

The same type of problem arises from the teacher's dual responsibility to the class and to each member in disciplining pupils for misconduct. Should the teacher act on the ethically justifiable premise that punishment should apply across the board and be commensurate with the offense, intending to prevent similar misconduct in the future, that strategy will prove ineffective some of the time because it ignores the personal reasons prompting the misconduct that vary with the individual.

Yet dealing with the offender rather than the offense, doing "right" by each pupil, makes the teacher look arbitrary—playing favorites—because children distinguish most readily between hard and soft punishments for the same misdeed and may not accept the teacher's perspective about what works and what is good for the individual child.

Sanctions, particularly negative ones, are especially problematic (over and above the question of whether rewards are rewarding and punishments punishing), because the relationship between teachers and pupils is one of long-term continuity. A teacher cannot punish a misdeed the way a policeman can issue a ticket for a traffic offense. Classroom events are not isolated in time; their future ramifications are often unpredictable—or at least unpredicted—but have a way of cropping up later, often with untoward consequences. More than setting precedents is involved. The teacher's armory of sanctions is not well-stocked; the conventional rewards of praise and good grades work best with pupils who value them and see schooling and its symbols as relevant preparation for their occupational careers. But those rewards may prove embarrassing to those by whom the school is suffered or the rewards may be seen as leading nowhere.

On the negative side, punishments have a way of yielding diminishing returns over the long run. Draconian punishments are illegal in many school systems, and there is little evidence that they contribute to the educational enterprise anyway. For many pupils, especially those for whom school is neither an unalloyed pleasure nor the road to worthwhile occupational destinations, less severe punishments can often be endured; they may be preferred (along with the acts provoking them) to the tedium of many classrooms. Over time, they may cease to be punishing and have little or no effect in achieving the outcome the teacher wants. And once a pupil has endured the worst a teacher can dish out, there is little the teacher can do beyond living with a bad situation. Severe punishments early in the game can have two very different outcomes: establish the teacher as one who means business or as one who has shot his wad. We do not know the conditions under which one outcome or the other ensues.

Implications of Time

Perhaps the real difficulty here is how we formulate the problem; it may be poor *conceptual* strategy to bootleg the ideas of "reward" and "punishment" from classical learning theory, tied as it is to transitory events, into a setting such as the classroom, a historical phenomenon. We might have to make our thinking about authority more appropriate to the problem of managing an enterprise over time, so that action at one time and under given conditions can be understood in terms of future contingencies and the conditions likely to surround them. The issue is joined precisely by Philip Jackson: "The teacher's compliment [a reward in the conventional scheme of things] is intended to entice the student (and those who are listening) to engage in certain behaviors *in the future*, but not simply in the repeated exposure of the knowledge he has just displayed" [9]; and also by Louis Smith and William Geoffrey, who treat the problem of compliance not as the rewarding and punishing of discrete acts but as establishing routines of trivial and important events, from which pupils can infer which of them require the teacher's authorization and which do not. Once they have introduced the element of time into the formulation of classroom events, it is no surprise to find them discussing strategies for attaining long-term compliance in terms of preparation for contingencies, provisional tries, pacing, and getting off the hook,[10] all of which depict teachers as governing their present action in the light of future events.

Implications of Grade Level

For reasons that escape me, striking organizational differences between elementary and secondary schools, especially when seen in temporal relationship to the family, have been sorely neglected. Perhaps because it is so obvious that most elementary teachers are women and that most high schools are departmentalized, we fail to recognize that there is more to say. The conventional wisdom has it that elementary teachers in the earliest grades are mother-surrogates. Yet either that contention is ill-conceived or my experience

---

[9] Philip W. Jackson. *Life in Classrooms.* New York: Holt, Rinehart and Winston, Inc., 1968. p. 24. (My italics.)

[10] Louis M. Smith and William Geoffrey. *The Complexities of an Urban Classroom.* New York: Holt, Rinehart and Winston, Inc., 1968. pp. 67-72, 96-121.

has been overly narrow. I do not know any mothers with 25 or more children—of about the same age. Although the prevalence of women as elementary teachers suggests continuity between family and school, particularly in the exercise of a personal, warm, and nurturant kind of authority—at least part of the time—and probably with respect to the problem of establishing good will, differences in the number of children and in age homogeneity characteristics of families and classrooms make the surrogate notion incomplete and inadequate. Because classrooms contain on the average about 30 like-aged children, teachers *cannot* exercise authority the same way parents do, even though the adult women in each setting may be motivated by similar impulses. Impersonality is bound to enter the classroom, given its collective properties. By implication, the elementary classroom provides conditions for children learning how to participate in new, more impersonal types of authority relationships. And the comparison with the family brings into relief both the elements of continuity (the woman in charge) and of discontinuity (the large number of like-aged children).

Children's passage through school from the elementary through the secondary years involves an annual progression through grades. Crossing each grade boundary requires that the child sever his relationship with last year's teacher and establish a new one with his current teacher. Although the principles of authority do not change appreciably during the elementary years, the progression through grades, with its associated change of teachers, provides children with the opportunity to infer that "teacher" is distinct from the particular person teaching. To put it more abstractly, the child can learn that persons and social positions are not equivalent. He has a teacher every year, but it is a different person; and where the school provides for the systematic variation of persons and positions, the family does not. In the usual course of events, the child's parents remain the same. For this reason, the family is less well suited, by virtue of the experiences it provides and fails to provide, for children to learn the difference between persons and positions.

Secondary schools are departmentalized by subject matter, and have about equal numbers of men and women teachers. These are hardly earth-shaking observations, but their implications for authority should not be ignored. There are many criteria for departmentalizing organizations, but the division of labor in secondary schools follows lines of specialized expertise. Although teachers have a general aura of authority because they are adults among children and because they occupy a position in the school to which certain powers and prerogatives are assigned by law and by school system rules, they also exercise a kind of authority based on their claim to mastery over a specific area of learning. English teachers, for example, do not teach mathematics, nor are they supposed to. When assigned to do so by administrators, they gladly express their displeasure on grounds of incompetence. Moreover, their training prepares them to teach a subject (at the secondary level, to be sure), but not to become secondary school teachers in general. By contrast, elementary school teachers are trained to become elementary school teachers.

While some subjects tend to attract more men and others more women, the sex of teachers remains independent of the subject taught. Competence in the subject, then, is the primary consideration in secondary teaching assignments, and this represents a departure from the elementary school as far as sex is concerned. In other words, women are assigned to teach in secondary schools for the same reasons as men, not because they have nurturant inclinations imputed to them as do their elementary school counterparts.

If we compare the secondary school with the elementary school and the family, the most conspicuous difference lies in the identification of a new *principle* of authority: expertness, or specific competence. This does not mean that parents and elementary teachers are incompetent or lack expertness; it does mean, however, that secondary schools are so organized that the competence dimension of authority can be socially distinguished from adulthood in general, from generation, from superordination, and from sex, all or some of which are combined indistinguishably in earlier relationships of authority. From the pupils' vantage point, secondary schooling affords them opportunities, presented to them systematically, to discover that compliance is expected by virtue of superiority gained through the mastery of specific skills. Whatever the skill in question, an expert demonstrates that he can do it better, and by so doing can gain respect.

Piece by piece, I have tried to argue that the experience of schooling, and especially the sequence of events beginning with family life and proceeding through elementary and secondary schools, provides social settings in which *aspects* of authority relationships typically found in adult life can be learned. Yet this contention must be taken with some caution. First, I have argued that children learn about authority by inference based on their experiences in social settings having certain structural properties. This is an assumption that lacks systematic verification; but we do need a place to start. Second, I can only posit the conditions from which inferences can be made but cannot demonstrate that they *are* made and by which pupils.

We all know that many pupils do not accept the premises of the school regime and reject its prevailing principles of authority. Any decent hypothesis designed to explain how principles of authority *are* acquired must also explain why they are not. With these cautions in mind, schooling appears to produce several outcomes: elements of equality and impersonality (both related to the collective nature of classrooms and the increasing ratios of children to adults through the family-elementary school-secondary school sequence); the distinction between persons and social positions (related to the crossing of grade boundaries); the principle of authority based on expertise (related to the departmentalization of secondary schools); and the specification of conditions under which personal, impersonal, and expert principles of authority are appropriate (related to the separation of schooling from the family and to the sequence of school levels).

What Is Learned About Authority: Outcomes of Schooling

An early childhood formulation of how children learn the principles and conduct of authority relationships leaves an uncomfortably large number of phenomena unexplained. If a child learns to respond to parental authority based on strong emotional bonds, close personal attachment, and dependency, why does he not generalize the familial experience to all other authority relationships? Or, to what extent does he generalize, and under what conditions? If schools are organized on different principles of authority than families (and there is reason to believe they are) and provide inducements for learning those principles (and it appears they can), should not children also learn the principles appropriate for getting along in school?

If principles of authority vary in appropriateness from one situation to another, how do children learn to match principles with circumstances? There is something wrong, for example, if people confuse their employers with their fathers. Through what sequence of events and conditions do young people acquire the psychological capacities and adopt the patterns of conduct to participate in the *various* kinds of authority relationships that adult life entails? Since the retrospective, early childhood formulation does not speak to these questions, perhaps we can benefit from a prospective one that links stages of schooling with conditions of adult life. Although the historical question of how the linkage between schools and other non-familial institutions—economic, political, religious—developed is clearly beyond the scope of this discussion, we can nevertheless observe the continuities and discontinuities in the social organization of families, schools, and those institutions that engage our thoughts and energies as adults.

Workers and Clients

What, then, does adult life demand of us, and in what ways does schooling contribute to meeting its demands? Stated this way, the questions are unmanageably broad; therefore, I limit myself here to two facets of occupational life: situations of authority arising in occupational pursuits, and those arising when we deal with others engaged in *their* occupational pursuits. That is, I am concerned with people at work and as the "clients" of others at work, and ignore the parental, political, religious, and leisure time facets of their lives, as well as others, though not because they are any less important.

Consider the ostensibly trivial example of a corporation executive buying a tie at a clothing store. At first glance, this episode does not look as if it involves authority at all; but only because the principles underlying it are seldom challenged does it look like an illustration of routine exchange. The situation involves two relationships entailing elements of authority: between the salesman and his employer (the latter unmentioned in the description but nevertheless there); and between the salesman and the customer. The first is a hierarchical relationship of employment established through a labor contract that binds the employee to act in certain ways: sell ties, attract business, be courteous, work a certain number of days and hours, and comply with the employer's directives as long as they fall within agreed-upon limits. For his part, the employer is obligated to pay wages and fringe benefits at agreed-upon rates, maintain working conditions at acceptable standards, and if a union is involved, adhere to the rules of grievance procedures and the like. The employee can quit and the employer can fire under certain circumstances. This surely is a bare-bones description of the contractual side of employment; but it is not meant to be complete, only to contain certain elements of the relationship.

Between salesman and customer, the hierarchical aspects of the relationship are less clear-cut. The salesman exercises authority to the extent that he controls the transaction (through power gained by employment); he will not relinquish the tie unless payment is forthcoming, this despite the fact that the buyer is likely to be wealthier and capable of exercising far greater power in the larger economy. That is, he has more of the trappings conventionally associated with authority, *but they do not pertain to this situation.* He does, however, have the right to take action against the salesman through his employer should the salesman fail to meet his obligations in the commercial exchange. But additional considerations enter the relationships among buyer, seller, and employer pertaining to the sale of a tie.

First, all those involved assent to general societal rules that apply to buying, selling, and employing that are not negotiable at each sale.[11] Second, the salesman would sell to anyone who could pay the price, and the purchaser could buy from any salesman. Similarly, the employer could hire any salesman as long as he had the necessary competence and personal qualities, and the salesman could work for any employer as long as the pay and the working conditions were satisfactory. Third, the subordinate in each pair of relationships has the right to apply sanctions should his respective superior fail to meet his obligations; that is, the legitimate power of subordinates distinguishes relationships of authority from those of personal submission. Fourth, the rights of each superior derive from general rules of conduct they adhere to and from the subordinate's acknowledgment of the validity of those rules. Thus, we have a complex phenomenon whose elements can be formulated abstractly and extended to a variety of apparently different situations. Even the two relationships under consideration differ, if for no other reason than that one is transitory and the other endures.

Elements in Authority Relationships

I took this example because it illustrates two kinds of authority about as remote as one can find from that prevailing in families; and while they look commonplace, they nevertheless conceal the problem of how people acquire the psychological capacities to participate in relationships that make such different demands on them.

[11] These are the non-contractual elements of contract that Durkheim wrote about in *The Division of Labor in Society.*

But what are the main elements in the relationships involved in the sale of a tie?

1. Impersonality: It makes no difference which *particular* individuals are involved as long as they have the required attributes and resources: money, and both the technical and personal capacities necessary to buy, sell, and establish contractual agreements.[12]

2. The situation: The conduct of the men (as well as a set of beliefs and norms left implicit) typically appears not only in this constellation of exchange and employment but in others like it (for example, boarding a bus, bringing wash to the laundry, or taking out a mortgage). The men did not act as if they were parent and child, lawyer and client, doctor and patient, clergyman and parishioner, each of which constitutes a relationship of authority predicated on its own peculiar principles. The situation, in effect, "defines" the boundaries that separate appropriate and inappropriate conduct; in addition, the criteria of appropriateness are known.

3. Legitimacy: By definition, all authority relationships are based on some principle of legitimacy. Whenever compliance is at stake, a subordinate can ask, "Why should I do it?" That part of a superior's reply justifying compliance *is* the principle of legitimacy. The shared acknowledgment of that principle and of the superior's right to sanction distinguishes authority from coercion. In professional-client relationships, legitimacy derives from expertness; in the military, officers give orders based on powers associated with the position they occupy in a hierarchy and on rules assigning power to the position. In my commercial illustration, the salesman's authority is based on rules governing his obligations as an employee and on societal norms governing contractual exchange in the marketplace.

4. The social position: Although two people are directly engaged in the sale of the tie (more people are engaged indirectly), they do not bring their whole repertoire of human responses, senti-

---

[12] Lest there be any doubt that these capacities are far more than trivial and that they are learned, consider the case of Israeli bus drivers who must teach North African and Middle Eastern immigrants, who come steeped in a commercial tradition of haggling over the price, that bus fares are fixed and that schedules, not the driver's whim or self-interest, determine the time of departure. Elihu Katz and S. N. Eisenstadt. "Some Sociological Observations on the Response of Israeli Organizations to New Immigrants." *Administrative Science Quarterly* 5 (1): 123-26; 1960.

ments, and expressions into it. Commercial exchanges of this kind as well as the more enduring relationship of employment allow for a range of personal expression and individual idiosyncracy; the conduct of each man conforms to principles applying to buyers and sellers, employers and employees in general. A "buyer," for example, is not a person even though a person buys; it is a social position defined by its reciprocal bond with another position (a "seller") and is analytically independent of the particular person who buys. Whoever occupies the position characteristically conducts himself in ways that conform to norms of commercial exchange, whatever else he is capable of doing, feeling, and thinking in other situations. All a person needs to become a buyer, in addition to having enough money, are the psychological capacities to participate in impersonal relationships, understand the difference between persons and positions, distinguish between superiors and subordinates, identify the situations in which one type of conduct is more appropriate than another, and act accordingly. The same is true for employers and employees as well as for other relationships of authority, any one of which I might have chosen.

Experiences and Opportunities

What, then, is the connection between schooling and the capacities of adults to participate in authority relationships? As I have argued earlier, the structural arrangements of schools provide reasonably enduring and systematic experiences from which pupils *can* infer—not necessarily that they will—that acting impersonally, distinguishing between persons and positions, and recognizing different principles of legitimacy and authority are appropriately associated with particular situations related to grade, school level, and subject matter. But schools keep pupils in subordinate positions, and it is therefore debatable whether pupils' experiences provide them a good opportunity to acquire the capacities necessary to participate adequately as superordinates even if the inferences they make cover both facets of the relationship. Observers have said about Americans that they frequently have difficulty acting in superordinate positions: as bosses, supervisors, managers, and the like. Although this characteristic has usually been attributed to the widespread acceptance of an egalitarian ideology, it might just as plausibly be explained by the fact that schools provide children with few opportunities to act as superordinates. Instruction of younger pupils by older ones might help redress the balance.

Throughout I have hedged my contentions about the impact of schooling by stating that schools provide experiences and opportunities, not that pupils learn. Whether pupils actually learn from the available opportunities is debatable simply because there is more to school than experiences derived from structural arrangements. One consideration is whether schools provide adequate inducements for pupils to make the inferences and to act according to them. For example, a classroom is a public arena in which pupils' successes and failures readily become and remain public knowledge.[13] The stakes are personal self-respect when one's actions are continuously subject to public scrutiny and judgment; and since schools operate according to achievement standards which inherently produce winners and losers, the consistent loser will find little incentive to accept the school's message.

Similarly, though structural arrangements are fairly constant from school to school (at each level), the conduct of teachers varies considerably. Accordingly, one would expect pupils to discover a wide range of strategies for dealing with the constants and variables of the school regime: complying, withdrawing, cheating, seeking special attention, rebelling, any one of which can produce outcomes different from those expected, given only the structural characteristics of schools. Yet we know that many people learn to cope with the demands that authority relationships impose on them as adults; and there is good reason to believe that they did not acquire all the necessary capacities from their families, their adolescent peer groups, or the mass media. Hence, it is important to look at the schools in search of their contribution, a contribution based on an inferential linkage between structural arrangements and some of the elements of authority.

[13] For a graphic description of public vilification, see: Jules Henry. *Culture Against Man*. New York: Random House, Inc., 1963. pp. 295-305.

The Moral Atmosphere of the School

LAWRENCE KOHLBERG

I HAVE to start by saying that Philip Jackson* is responsible for my paper, by which I mean he is "to blame."

First, he is responsible because he invented the term "hidden" or "unstudied curriculum" to refer to 90 percent of what goes on in classrooms. Second, he is responsible because he induced me to speak about the unstudied curriculum when my only qualification to do so is that I have never studied it. While I have done plenty of observing of children in and out of classrooms, such observation has always been with reference to developing personality and behavior, and not in terms of the nature of classroom life and its influence on children. Third, he is to blame because he wrote a book defining the hidden curriculum on which I based this paper, and then he prepared a document, appearing in this booklet, defining the unstudied curriculum in a completely different way, leaving me holding the bag.

The Hidden Curriculum and Moral Education

Anyhow, I am going to revenge myself on Dr. Jackson for putting me in this awkward spot by claiming that I am the only person who is really an intellectual expert on this problem of the hidden curriculum. I say this because it will be my claim that the only integrated way of thinking about the hidden curriculum is to think of it as moral education, a topic about which few other academicians besides myself are currently concerned. To make

* Dr. Philip Jackson, Chairman, ASCD Elementary Education Council.

educational sense out of the insights of Jackson, Dreeben, Friedenberg, and Rosenthal, I shall claim, you must put them in the framework of the ideas and concerns in *moral* education propounded by such writers as Emile Durkheim, John Dewey, and Jean Piaget.

To make my point, I shall start with the central question most of us have about the hidden curriculum, that of whether it educates, miseducates, or does neither. I shall claim that the answer to this question depends upon a viable conception of moral development. The question itself, that of whether the hidden curriculum educates, is posed by the very phrase, "hidden curriculum." The phrase indicates that children are learning much in school that is not formal curriculum, and the phrase also asks whether such learning is truly educative.

In *Life in Classrooms*, Philip Jackson summarizes three central characteristics of school life: the crowds, the praise, and the power. Learning to live in the classroom means, first, learning to live and to be treated as a member of a crowd of same-age, same-status others.

Second, learning to live in the classroom means learning to live in a world in which there is impersonal authority, in which a relative stranger gives orders and wields power. Robert Dreeben emphasizes similar characteristics, first and foremost learning to live with authority. Both Jackson and Dreeben stress the fact that the hidden curriculum provides a way station between the personal relations of the family and the impersonal achievement and authority-oriented roles of adult occupational and sociopolitical life.

The perspectives of Jackson and Dreeben derive from a long and great tradition of educational sociology founded by Emile Durkheim in France at the end of the 19th century. According to Durkheim:

There is a great distance between the state in which the child finds himself as he leaves the family and the one toward which he must strive. Intermediaries are necessary, the school environment the most desirable. It is more extensive than the family or the group of friends. It results neither from blood nor free choice but from a meeting among subjects of similar age and condition. In that sense, it resembles political society. On the other hand it is limited enough so that personal relations can crystallize. It is groups of young persons more or less like those of the social system of the school which have enabled the formation of societies larger than the family. Even in simple societies without schools, the elders would assemble the group at a given age and initiate them collectively into the moral and intellectual patrimony of the group.

Induction into the moral patrimony of the group has never been conducted entirely within the family.[1]

What this sociological tradition of Durkheim and Dreeben is telling us is that you cannot get rid of authority in the classroom, because you need people who can live with it in the bigger society. Edgar Friedenberg starts out with the same Durkheim perspective before turning it on its ear. I hesitate to restate Dr. Friedenberg. I am tempted to say that he is the only person in the world who can state a message in many syllables, and make it come across with one-syllable impact. In *Coming of Age in America* Friedenberg says,

> After the family the school is the first social institution an individual must deal with, the place in which he learns to handle himself with strangers. Free societies depend upon their members to learn early and thoroughly that public authority is not like that of the family, but must rely basically on the impersonal application of general formulae.[2]

However, Friedenberg's observations of the hidden curriculum suggest that it is less a vehicle of socialization into a free society than that caricature of socialization we call a jail. Says Friedenberg:

> Between classes at Milgrim High, no student may walk down the corridor without a form signed by a teacher, telling where he is coming from, where he is going, and the time to the minute at which the pass is valid. There is no physical freedom whatever in Milgrim, there is no time or place in which a student may simply go about his business. Privacy is strictly forbidden. Toilets are locked. There are more different washrooms than there must have been in the Confederate Navy.[3]

Friedenberg's style of observation of the hidden curriculum is colored by his view that its function of socialization into large-scale society means socialization into a mass middle-class society of mediocrity, banality, and conformity. From this point of view, the hidden curriculum consists of "the ways in which education subverts the highest function of education, which is to help people understand the meaning of their lives and those of others."

I have summarized utterances by our other speakers to indicate how the perceived nature of the hidden curriculum rests on a prior perspective which is both a social theory and a mode of valuing.

---

[1] Emile Durkheim. *Moral Education.* New York: The Free Press, Inc., 1961. p. 231.

[2] Edgar Z. Friedenberg. *Coming of Age in America. Growth and Acquiescence.* New York: Random House, Inc., 1963. p. 43.

[3] *Ibid.*, p. 29.

The fact that this must necessarily be the case in social inquiry, I learned in an illuminating course by Edgar Friedenberg on social science method. The observation and study of a reading curriculum rest on assumptions of both what reading is and what reading as a desirable skill ought to be. The same is true of the hidden curriculum.

Educational Consequences of Moral Education

As the educational philosopher R. S. Peters points out, "the concept 'education' has built into it the criterion that something worthwhile should be achieved. It implies something worthwhile is being transmitted in a morally acceptable manner."[4] To discuss the educational consequences of the hidden curriculum is to discuss whether it does or can lead to the transmission of something worthwhile in a morally acceptable manner. While Friedenberg assumes this, Dreeben claims a value-neutral stance. Dreeben concludes an earlier article by saying,

The argument of this paper presents a formulation of how schooling contributes to the emergence of certain psychological outcomes, not to provide an apology or justification for these outcomes on ideological grounds. From the viewpoint of ideological justification, the process of schooling is problematic in that outcomes morally desirable from one perspective are undesirable from another.[5]

It is hard to understand what conclusions to draw from Dreeben's analysis if it is really value-neutral. The analysis points out that authority is necessary in adult society, so it is necessary to have a hidden curriculum by which it is learned in the school.

Nature of School Discipline

If Dreeben's analysis has real educational force, however, it is contained in the implicit value-perspective of functional sociology, the perspective that the invisible hand of societal survival guides the shaping of human institutions and gives them a value or wisdom not apparent at first glance. Durkheim, the founder of functional sociology, understood that functional sociology was not a value-free

[4] R. S. Peters. *Ethics and Education.* Chicago: Scott, Foresman and Company, 1967. p. 6.

[5] Robert Dreeben. "The Contribution of Schooling to the Learning of Norms." *Harvard Educational Review* 37 (2): 211-37; Spring 1967.

position, but essentially represented a moral point of view. Durkheim articulately and explicitly argued that the sociologist's definition of the invisible hand of the social system was also the definition of rational or scientific morality. So Durkheim goes further than saying that acceptance of authority is one of the key elements of the child's moral development.

Durkheim argues that the crowds, the praise, and the power which look so wasteful from the point of view of intellectual development are the necessary conditions for the moral development of the child. According to Durkheim,

Morality is respect for rule and is altruistic attachment to the social group. . . . although family education is an excellent preparation for the moral life, its usefulness is restricted, above all with respect to the spirit of discipline. That which is essential to the spirit of discipline, respect for the rule, can scarcely develop in the familial setting, which is not subject to general impersonal immutable regulation, and should have an air of freedom. But the child must learn respect for the rule; he must learn to do his duty because it is his duty, even though the task may not seem an easy one.

Such an apprenticeship must devolve upon the school. Too often, it is true, people conceive of school discipline so as to preclude endowing it with such an important moral function. Some see in it a simple way of guaranteeing superficial peace and order in the class. Under such conditions, one can quite reasonably come to view these imperative requirements as barbarous, as a tyranny of complicated rules. In reality, however, school discipline is not a simple device for securing superficial peace in the classroom; it is the morality of the classroom as a small society.[6]

Durkheim's System

I shall not go into Durkheim's system of moral education in detail in this paper except to say it is, in my opinion, the most philosophically and scientifically comprehensive, clear, and workable approach to moral education extant. Its workability has been demonstrated not in France but in Soviet Russia, where it has been elaborated from the point of view of Marxist rather than Durkheimian sociology. Like Durkheim, the Russians hold that altruistic concern or sacrifice, like the sense of duty, is always basically directed toward the group rather than to another individual or to an abstract principle. Durkheim reasons that altruism is always sacrificing the self for something greater than the self, and another self can

[6] Emile Durkheim, *op. cit.*, p. 148.

never be greater than the self except as it stands for the group or for society. Accordingly a central part of moral education is the sense of belonging to, and sacrificing for, a group. Says Durkheim,

In order to commit ourselves to collective ends, we must have above all a feeling and affection for the collectivity. We have seen that such feelings cannot arise in the family where solidarity is based on blood and intimate relationship since the bonds uniting the citizens of a country have nothing to do with such relationships. The only way to instill the inclination to collective life is to get hold of the child when he leaves his family and enters school. We will succeed the more easily because in certain respects, he is more amenable to this joining of minds in a common consciousness than is the adult. To achieve this tonic effect on the child, the class must really share in a collective life. Such phrases as "the class," "the spirit of the class," and "the honor of the class" must become something more than abstract expressions in the student's mind. A means to awaken the feeling of solidarity is the discreet and deliberate use of collective punishments and rewards. Collective sanctions play a very important part in the life of the classroom. The most powerful means to instill in children the feeling of solidarity is to feel that the value of each is a function of the worth of all.[7]

A Russian Example

One of the logical but to us rather horrifying innovations in the hidden curriculum Durkheim suggests on this basis is the use of collective responsibility, collective punishment and reward. Here is how a Russian moral education manual (quoted by Urie Bronfenbrenner) tells us this and other aspects of moral education are to be done in a third-grade classroom:

Class 3-B is just an ordinary class; it's not especially well disciplined.

The teacher has led this class now for three years, and she has earned affection, respect, and acceptance as an authority from her pupils. Her word is law for them.

The bell has rung, but the teacher has not yet arrived. She has delayed deliberately in order to check how the class will conduct itself.

In the class all is quiet. After the noisy class break, it isn't so easy to mobilize yourself and to quell the restlessness within you! Two monitors at the desk silently observe the class. On their faces is reflected the full importance and seriousness of the job they are performing. But there is no need for them to make any reprimands: the youngsters with pleasure and pride maintain scrupulous discipline; they are proud

[7] *Ibid.*, p. 239.

of the fact that their class conducts itself in a manner that merits the confidence of the teacher. And when the teacher enters and quietly says be seated, all understand that she deliberately refrains from praising them for the quiet and order, since in their class it could not be otherwise.

During the lesson, the teacher gives an exceptional amount of attention to collective competition between "links." (The links are the smallest unit of the Communist youth organization at this age level.) Throughout the entire lesson the youngsters are constantly hearing which link has best prepared its lesson, which link has done the best at numbers, which is the most disciplined, which has turned in the best work.

The best link not only gets a verbal positive evaluation but receives the right to leave the classroom first during the break and to have its notebooks checked before the others. As a result the links receive the benefit of collective education, common responsibility, and mutual aid.

"What are you fooling around for? You're holding up the whole link," whispers Kolya to his neighbor during the preparation period for the lesson. And during the break he teaches her how better to organize her books and pads in her knapsack.

"Count more carefully," says Olya to her girl friend. "See, on account of you our link got behind today. You come to me and we'll count together at home."[8]

I do not need to say any more to indicate that Durkheim and the Russians know how to make the hidden curriculum explicit, and how to make it work. Furthermore, it is clear that Durkheim has simply taken to its logical conclusion a justification of the hidden curriculum which many teachers vaguely assume, the justification that the discipline of group life directly promotes moral character. We see, however, that when this line of thinking is carried to its logical conclusion, it leads to a definition of moral education as the promotion of collective national discipline which most of us feel is neither rational ethics nor the American constitutional tradition.

Valuing the Hidden Curriculum

What I am arguing is that the trouble with Durkheim's approach to the hidden curriculum is not that of starting from a conception of moral development, but of starting from a wrong conception of moral development. Before having the arrogance to present the right conception of moral development, I want to indicate briefly how analyses of the hidden curriculum which do

[8] Urie Bronfenbrenner. "Soviet Methods of Character Education, Some Implications for Research." *American Psychologist* 17: 550-65; 1962.

not articulate an explicit conception of the moral fail to provide a framework an educator can really get hold of. We have pointed out that Dreeben sees the hidden curriculum as shaped by the invisible hand of the social system without being willing to say whether what serves the social system is good or bad. In contrast, Friedenberg seems to see the hidden curriculum as shaped by pretty much the same invisible hand of society or lower-middle class society, but to see this invisible hand as bad, as destroying the hearts and minds of the poor, the aristocrats, and the non-middle class in general. The core difficulty of Friedenberg's analysis is his willingness to call things good or bad without systematic criteria of morality behind his judgments. This is reflected in the question, "If you don't like the values which dominate education, what set of values should dominate education?"

The core badness of the hidden curriculum, in Friedenberg's view, is its injustice, its violation of the rights and dignity of adolescents who do not meet the mass image. One might, therefore, expect Friedenberg to hold that the optimal moral consequence of a good curriculum would be the cultivation of just men, of the sense of justice. Instead he comes out for a bag of aristocratic virtues which are as arbitrary as the middle-class virtues he rejects. Put in different terms, he says, "Leave kids alone. Respect their freedom!" without asking whether an education that leaves them alone will educate them to respect the freedom of others.

The School—Transmitter of Values

If lack of explicitness in moral framework creates confusion in Friedenberg's analysis, Dreeben's and Jackson's moral neutrality presents worse puzzles in interpreting their cogent observations. For instance, Dreeben points out that the school arbitrarily demands independent performance on tasks while cooperation in tasks is considered a good thing under other circumstances. In school tests and assignments, cooperation is cheating, while it is legitimate on other occasions. Jackson makes a similar point.

Another course of action engaged in by most students at least some of the time is to disguise the failure to comply, that is, to cheat. Learning to make it in school involves, in part, learning how to falsify our behavior.[9]

[9] Philip Jackson. *Life in Classrooms*. New York: Holt, Rinehart and Winston, Inc., 1968. p. 27.

It is not quite correct to say, as Jackson does, that the hidden curriculum of the school teaches children to cheat. More accurately, the school teaches children about cheating and leads to the development of styles of approach to the issue of cheating. In functional sociology phrases, it prepares children for life in an industrial society in which they will have to decide where and when to cheat and when not to. Recent studies confirm the old findings of Hartshorne and May that schooling does not lead to increased honesty. In experimental situations allowing cheating, older children in a given school are as likely to cheat as younger children. What age and passage through school appear to do is to lead to more generalized strategies about cheating. Some older children are more likely to cheat all the time than younger children, while other older children are more likely to refrain from cheating altogether than younger children. This leaves the mean amount of cheating the same.

The point I am making is that Dreeben's analysis of the hidden curriculum suggests that it has neither the hidden nor the manifest function of developing morality. While it presents moral issues such as whether to cheat, its central norms are not moral norms but norms of independent competition and achievement. Accordingly while teachers may strive to police cheating, they will not exert any real influence over children's moral values or character. Put in a different way, Dreeben is telling us that the schools are transmitting values, but they are not what educators usually think are moral values. A good functional sociologist might reply that from the social system point of view, cultivating independent competition is more important or more *moral* than cultivating honesty, since our society is built to tolerate a lot of petty cheating but is not built to tolerate a lot of people who are not interested in making it by institutional achievement standards. It is just at this point that we have to go back to a conception of the moral before the implications of Dreeben's sociological analysis can be understood.

The Hidden Curriculum as Freedom

One final example of an approach to the hidden curriculum denies considering its use and value for moral education. This example is that of Summerhill's A. S. Neill, whose solution is to chuck out both the hidden curriculum and the concept of morality from education. Dreeben and Jackson say the hidden curriculum is authority, Neill says chuck it out and make the hidden curriculum freedom. Friedenberg's position seems not too different, if Friedenberg were to start a school as Neill has done. Says Neill,

> We set out to make a school in which we should allow children freedom to be themselves. To do this we had to renounce all discipline, all direction, all moral training. We have been called brave but it did not require courage, just a complete belief in the child as a good, not an evil, being. A child is innately wise and realistic. If left to himself without adult suggestion of any kind he will develop as far as he is capable of developing. I believe that it is moral instruction that makes the child bad, not good.[10]

A philosopher could while away a pleasant afternoon trying to find out just what ethical framework Neill is using when he says children are good but morality is bad. It is more instructive, however, to recognize that even at Summerhill moral problems arise and to see how Neill handles them. Some years ago, Neill says,

> We had two pupils arrive at the same time, a boy of seventeen and a girl of sixteen. They fell in love with each other and were always together. I met them late one night and stopped them. "I don't know what you two are doing," I said, "and morally I don't care for it isn't a moral question at all. But economically, I do care. If you, Kate, have a kid my school will be ruined. You have just come to Summerhill. To you it means freedom to do what you like. Naturally, you have no special feeling for the school. If you had been here from the age of seven, I'd never have had to mention the matter. You would have such a strong attachment to the school that you would think of the consequences to Summerhill.[11]

What the quotation makes clear, of course, is that the hidden moral curriculum of Summerhill is the explicit curriculum of Durkheim and the Russians. Unquestioned loyalty to the school, to the collectivity, seems to be the ultimate end of moral education at Summerhill. Surely, however, moral education has some other aims than a loyalty to the school and to other children which might possibly later transfer to loyalty to the nation and other men. To consider what such aims might be we may start with the observation that all the writers we have discussed so far have assumed that morality is fundamentally emotional and irrational. Neill, Dreeben, and Durkheim agree on this point, differing only in their evaluation

---

[10] A. S. Neill. *Summerhill: A Radical Approach to Child Rearing.* New York: Hart Publishing Company, Inc. Copyright 1960. p. 4. By permission.
[11] *Ibid.*, p. 57-58.

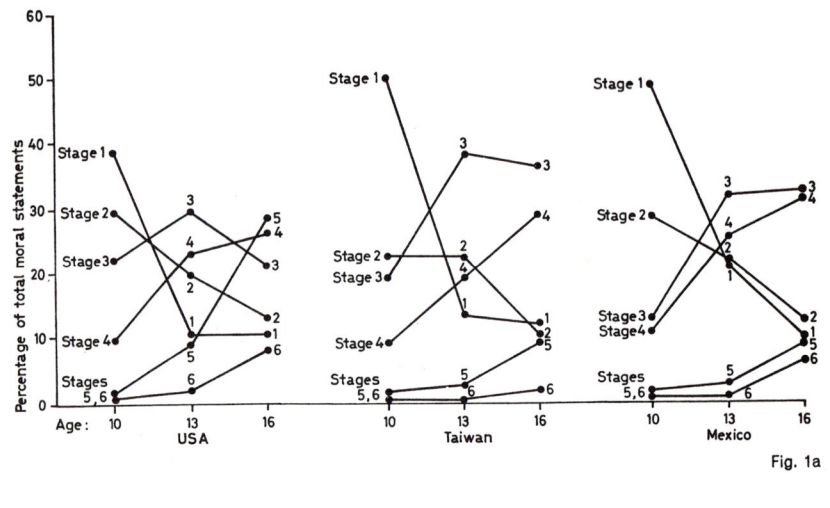

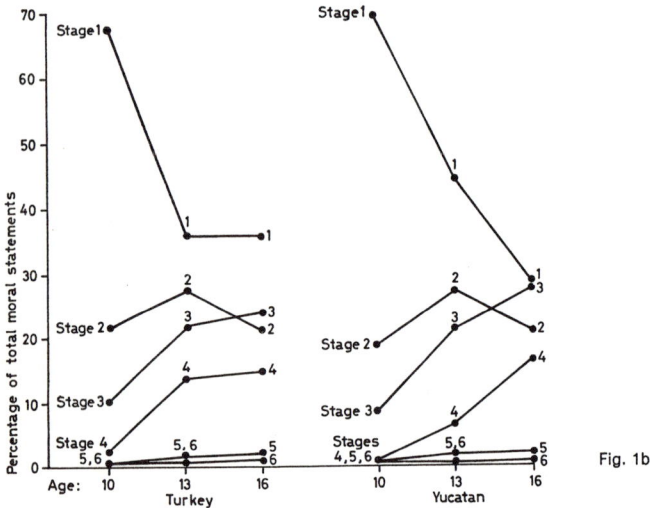

114   THE UNSTUDIED CURRICULUM: ITS IMPACT ON CHILDREN

Fig. 1a. Middle-class urban boys in the U.S., Taiwan and Mexico. At age 10 the stages are used according to difficulty. At age 13, Stage 3 is most used by all three groups. At age 16, U.S. boys have reversed the order of age 10 stages (with the exception of 6). In Taiwan and Mexico, conventional (3–4) stages prevail at age 16, with Stage 5 also little used.

Fig. 1b. Two isolated villages, one in Turkey, the other in Yucatan, show similar patterns in moral thinking. There is no reversal of order, and preconventional (1–2) does not gain a clear ascendancy over conventional stages at age 16.*

* Fig. 1a and 1b (above) and Fig. 2 (on page 116). L. Kohlberg and R. Kramer. "Continuities and Discontinuities in Childhood and Adult Moral Development." *Human Development* 12: 93-120; 1969. Basel, Switzerland: S. Karger Basel.

of the worth of this irrational part of life. It is assumed that the means and ends of intellectual education are one thing and those of moral education another.

Growth of Moral Character

Durkheim and Dreeben assume that learning to accept rules and authority is a concrete nonrational process based on repetition, emotion, and sometimes sanctions. The assumption is that the child is controlled by primitive and selfish drives he is reluctant to give up and that the steady experience of authority and discipline is necessary to live with rules. The notions of Dewey and Piaget, that the child genuinely learns to accept authority when he learns to understand and accept the reasons and principles behind the rules, leads moral education in a different direction, tied much more closely to the intellectual curriculum of the school. This second direction is supported by many research findings. My research and that of others indicates that the development of moral character is in large part a sequential progressive growth of basic principles of moral reasoning and their application to action.

Moral Stages

In my research, I have longitudinally followed the development of moral thinking of a group of 50 boys from age 10 to age 25, by asking them at each three-year interval how and why they would resolve a set of 11 moral dilemmas. We have found that changes in moral thinking go step by step through six stages, with children's development stopping or becoming fixed at any one of the six stages. These stages are defined in Table 1. (See p. 124.) We have found these same stages in the same order in children in Mexico, Turkey, England, and Taiwan, in illiterate villages, and in the urban middle and lower classes, as Figures 1 and 2 indicate.

Take one dilemma, such as whether a husband should steal a drug to save his dying wife if he could get it no other way. (Sample responses to the dilemma at each stage are presented in Table 2.) Stage 1 is obedience and punishment. You should not steal the drug because you will be put in jail. Stage 2 is pragmatic hedonism and exchange. Steal the drug, you need your wife and she may do the same for you someday. Stage 3 is love, happiness, kindness, and approval-oriented. Steal the drug because you want to be a good husband and good husbands love their wives. Stage 4 is the mainte-

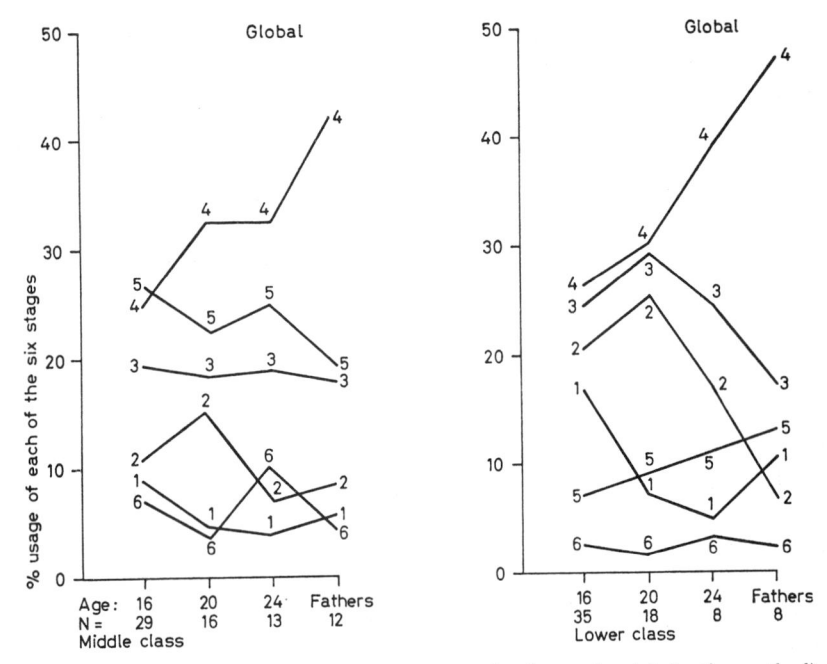

116   THE UNSTUDIED CURRICULUM: ITS IMPACT ON CHILDREN

Fig. 2. Moral judgment profiles (percentage usage of each stage by global rating method) for middle and lower class males at four ages. [From RICHARD KRAMER 'Changes in Moral Judgment Response Pattern During Late Adolescence and Young Adulthood' Ph. D. dissertation, University of Chicago, 1968].

nance of the social order, respect for law and order, and the loyalty to the group's goals, the morality of Durkheim and the Russians. Stage 5 is social-contract constitutionalism, the definition of the good as the welfare of society where society is conceived as a set of individuals with equal rights and where rules and obligations are formed by the contractual agreements of free men. Stage 6 is the sense of principled obligation to universal human values and justice even when these are not represented in particular legal agreements and contracts in our society.

Each stage includes the core values of the prior stage but defines them in a more universal, differentiated, and integrated form. To the Stage 4 mind of George Wallace, the concept of justice is a threat to law and order, because he does not really understand the concept of a constitutional democracy in which law and order, the government, is set up to pursue and preserve justice, the equal rights of free men; and in that sense the concept of justice includes the valid elements of the law and order concept.

Let me illustrate Stage 5 and its difference from Stage 6 by a quotation from Earl Kelley's pamphlet *Return to Democracy*.

A simple way to measure our efforts to educate is to judge them in the light of the tenets of democracy. . . . It is the way our forefathers decided that they wanted to live, and it is reaffirmed daily by all kinds of Americans except a very few who belong to the radical right or left. The founding fathers attempted to make the democratic ideal come to life by building our Constitution around these tenets. . . . (a) Every person has worth, has value. . . . He is entitled to be treated as a human being. He has equal rights under the law, without regard to his condition of birth or the circumstances under which he has been obliged to live. (b) The individual counts for everything. The state and school—constructed by individuals to serve individuals—are implementations of the way we want to live. . . . (c) Each individual is unique, different from any other person who has ever lived. . . . (d) Each individual has his own unique purposes, and these are the paths down which his energies can be best spent. (e) Freedom is a requirement for living in a democracy. . . . This does not mean freedom to do just as one pleases. Nobody has this right if he lives in the vicinity of any other human being, because the other human being has rights which also must be respected. . . . If we are to emphasize the learner himself, there can be no better point of reference than the democratic ideal. It has the advantage of having been agreed upon.[12]

Professor Kelley's statement is clearly not Stage 6, although it contains a recognition of universal human rights and of justice. Fundamentally, however, Kelley is arguing that his ideal springs from a ready-made agreed-upon social-constitutional framework, one which permits social change and individual differences, but one which derives its validity from the fact that it is agreed upon, and that it has worked, rather than from the intrinsic universality and morality of its principles. If a man is confronted with a choice of stealing a drug to save a human life, however, Kelley's framework provides no clear ethical solution.

If it is recognized, however, that universal respect for fundamental human rights and for the human personality provides a moral guide defining the way in which any human should act, as well as being the established underlying values of our particular society, we are on the way to Stage 6. It is quite likely that in his personal thinking about moral dilemmas, Kelley would operate in

---

[12] Earl Kelley. *Return to Democracy*. Washington, D.C.: American Association of Elementary/Kindergarten/Nursery Educators, National Education Association, Elementary Instructional Service, 1964.

a Stage 6 framework, but that in trying to write a public document that will gain agreement among members of a professional association, he turns to the safer ground of established actual agreement rather than that of Stage 6 principles which logically are universal though they may not be the basis of historical consensus.

For my purposes, it is not critical whether we take Stage 5 or Stage 6 as defining a desirable level for moral education in the schools. It can safely be said that lower-stage conceptions of morality cannot define the aims of moral education, because the Constitution forbids a type of moral education which involves indoctrination and violation of the rights of individuals and their families to freedom of beliefs. This prevents us from taking the beliefs of the majority as an aim of moral education in the schools, partly because the majority has no consensus on moral issues, partly because studies show majority beliefs are grounded more on Stage 3 beliefs in conforming virtues and Stage 4 conceptions of law and order than upon Stage 5 awareness of justice and constitutional democracy.

An example of a school principal who expressed the Stage 4 beliefs of the majority has been provided by Friedenberg. The principal told his high school students they could not have a radical speaker because the speaker was against the government and the school was an agency of the government. If he had understood our constitutional system at the Stage 5 level, he would have recognized that the school as an agent of the government has a responsibility for communicating conceptions of individual rights which the government was created to maintain and serve. I am not arguing that the principal had a Stage 6 moral obligation to defy heroically an angry community of parents to see that a given radical speaker was heard. He was failing as a moral educator, however, if all he could transmit was Stage 4 moral messages to students many of whom were quite likely already at a Stage 5 level. Let us assume that all of the readers of this paper are at Stage 5 or Stage 6. What should your moral messages to children be?

Moral Comprehension of Children

A series of carefully replicated experimental studies demonstrate that children seldom comprehend messages more than one stage above their own, and understand but reject messages below their own level (Turiel, 1969). The studies also indicate that people can comprehend and to some extent use all stages lower than their own. As principled moral educators, you have the capacity to use lower level as well as higher level messages when you choose.

With young children, it is clear that we can make the mistake of both too high and too low a level. It is worse to make the mistake of being at too low a level because the child loses respect for the message in that case. Yet this is frequently the case. Let me quote an example of a familiar tone of Stage 3, "everything nice," from a magazine called *Wee Wisdom: A Character Building Magazine:*

> "Thank you" can just be a polite little word or it can be something warm and wonderful and happy that makes your heart sing. As Boosters let us climb the steps of appreciation on a golden stairway. Let us add that magic ingredient to all our thank yous. Everyone is happier when our thanks express real appreciation.
>
> Won't you join the boosters to climb the stairway to happiness and success. What a wonderful world it will be if we all do our part.[13]

The quotation is of course straight Stage 3, be nice and everyone will be happy. The only person who can sell that message to adolescents is Tiny Tim and he has to adopt a few unusual mannerisms to do so.

It is, of course, quite necessary to transmit moral messages at Stages 3 and 4 in the elementary school years. Even here, however, it is probably desirable to have these messages under the integrative control of higher levels. Holstein (1968) studies a group of middle-class 12-year-olds who were about equally divided between the preconventional (Stages 1 and 2) and the conventional (Stages 3 and 4) level.

Principled mothers were more likely to have conventional-level children than conventional mothers. The principled mothers were capable of conventional moral messages and undoubtedly emitted them. However, their integration of them in terms of the higher level made them better moral educators even where the moral educator's task is bringing children to the conventional level.

Developing Moral Education

My research has led my colleagues and me to go on to develop experimental programs of moral education from the intellectual side. Programs center around the discussion of real and hypothetical moral conflicts. We set up arguments between students at

[13] *Wee Wisdom—A Character Building Magazine.* June 1967. p. 83.

one stage and those at the next stage up, since children are able to assimilate moral thinking only one stage above their own. The preliminary results have been encouraging, with most students advancing one stage and maintaining the advance a year later in comparison with a control group (Blatt and Kohlberg, 1969). Such procedures form an explicit intellectual curriculum of moral education. Such a curriculum should not exist in abstraction; however, it should exist as a reflection upon the hidden curriculum of school life.

What is the essential nature of the hidden curriculum as a vehicle of moral growth? Our viewpoint accepts as inevitable the crowds, the praise, and the power which the school inevitably contains. How much or little crowd, praise, or discipline, or power is of little interest from our point of view. A generation of child psychology research measuring the effects of amount and type of family authority and discipline on moral character have yielded few substantial results. If these things do not define the moral-educational effects of the family, they are unlikely to define the weaker and more transient moral effects of particular schools.

The Role of the Teacher

We believe what matters in the hidden curriculum is the moral character and ideology of the teachers and principal as these are translated into a working social atmosphere which influences that atmosphere of the children. In the introduction of a recent book presenting portraits of Shapiro, the principal of P.S. 119, and Boyden, the headmaster of Deerfield, Mayerson says, "Each is engaged in a diligent attempt to achieve a consistency between an articulated personal morality and the daily passage of their lives. The two schools are the sites of the working out of this ideal." [14] Shapiro, the Harlem principal, was trained as a clinical psychologist. His ideology is one of empathy, permissiveness, and respect for his deprived children: meeting their needs, trying to keep their liveliness from dying, with no explicit concern for moral education. The ideology is one of warmth and humility and Shapiro is a warm and humble man who is against the crowds, the praise, and the

[14] Nat Hentoff. *Our Children Are Dying;* and John A. McPhee. *The Headmaster: Frank L. Boyden, of Deerfield.* Two books in one volume with an introduction by Charlotte Mayerson. New York: Four Winds Press, Inc., 1966. p. 8.

power. How does his ideology, his warmth, and his humility come across to the school? I quote,

> A woman announced that the assembly was being dedicated to Dr. Shapiro. He winced. Eleven girls stood and sang in unison: "Oh he is the bravest, Oh he is the greatest, we'll fight before we switch."
> "Talk about brainwashing," Shapiro mumbled, slumped in a back row seat.[15]

It is clear that this humble and dedicated believer in permissiveness is in firm control of the crowds, the praise, and the power.

Neill's personal characteristics are quite different from Shapiro's, yet he too has created an effective moral atmosphere. As a character, Neill is obviously dogmatic, self-assured, imposing. One could not want a stronger, more vigorous leader of a *leaderless* school. In character, he is reminiscent of Frank Boyden, the headmaster of Deerfield, who is described as being without contradiction humanitarian, ruthless, loyal, selfish, selfless, stubborn, indestructible, and infallible. Unlike Neill, Boyden believes in discipline and believes that the purpose of his school is moral character building. Like Neill, Boyden radiates a belief in the value of his school as an end in itself.

In citing Boyden, Shapiro, and Neill as masters of the hidden curriculum, I have tried to indicate that the transformation of the hidden curriculum into a moral atmosphere is not a matter of one or another educational technique or ideology or means, but a matter of the moral energy of the educator, of his communicated belief that his school or classroom has a human purpose. To get his message across, he may use permissiveness or he may use discipline, but the effective moral educator has a believable human message.

The Ends of Moral Education

We have seen, however, that this human message cannot be an ideology of education, or it will end by treating the school as the ultimate value, with the corresponding eventual morality of loyalty to the school or to an ideological doctrine of education in itself. The hidden curriculum of the school must represent something more than the goals and social order of the school itself. Our definition of moral maturity as the principled sense of justice suggests what this end must be. The teaching of justice requires just schools.

[15] *Ibid.*, p. 38.

The crowds, the praise, and the power are neither just nor unjust in themselves. As they are typically used in the schools, they represent the values of social order and of individual competitive achievement. The problem is not to get rid of the praise, the power, the order, and the competitive achievement, but to establish a more basic context of justice which gives them meaning. In our society authority derives from justice, and in our society learning to live with authority should derive from and aid learning to understand and to feel justice.

The need to make the hidden curriculum an atmosphere of justice, and to make this hidden curriculum explicit in intellectual and verbal discussions of justice and morality, is becoming more and more urgent. Our research studies have shown that our Stage 6 or most morally mature college students are the students most active in support of universal civil rights and in support of the universal sacredness of human life as both issues have recently come in clear conflict with authority, law and order, national loyalty, and college administrations. Research also indicates that these mature adolescents are joined by an immature group of rebellious egoistic relativists who think justice means everyone "doing his thing." It seems clear that student-administration confrontations will spread to younger and younger groups who are increasingly confused and immature in their thought about the issues of justice involved.

In the current college confrontations, it has been typical for administrators to harden into poses of what I call Stage 4 law and order thinking, or what I call Stage 5 social contract legalism. What else can they do? What else are they taught in programs of school administration? This is hard to answer because the world's great moral educators have not run schools. Moral education is something of a revolutionary activity. When Socrates engaged in genuine moral education, he was executed for corrupting the Athenian youth. I mention Socrates to indicate that it is not only America who kills its moral educators, its men like Martin Luther King, Jr., who both talked and lived as drum majors of justice.

These fatalities and many others will continue to go on as long as the dialogue about justice goes on across the barricades. The current fate of the school administrator is to find that if he keeps the dialogue out of the classroom, he will face it across the barricades with students to whom he cannot speak. The educational use of the hidden curriculum is not to prevent the dialogue by calling classroom law and order moral character, nor to cast it out on the ground that the child needs only freedom, but to use it to bring the dialogue of justice into the classroom. It is my hope that our educational research program may find worthwhile ways of doing this in the next five years. It is perhaps less a hope than a dream that the American schools will want to use it.

References

M. Blatt and Lawrence Kohlberg. "The Effects of a Classroom Discussion Program upon the Moral Levels of Preadolescents." Accepted for publication in revised form for *Merrill Palmer Quarterly.* 1969. (In preparation.)

Urie Bronfenbrenner. "Soviet Methods of Character Education, Some Implications for Research." *American Psychologist* 17: 550-65; 1962.

John Dewey. *Moral Principles in Education.* Boston: Houghton Mifflin Company, 1909.

Robert Dreeben. "The Contribution of Schooling to the Learning of Norms." *Harvard Educational Review* 37 (2): 211-37; Spring 1967.

Robert Dreeben. *On What Is Learned in School.* Reading, Massachusetts: Addison-Wesley Publishing Company, Inc., 1968.

Emile Durkheim. *Moral Education.* New York: The Free Press, Inc., 1961. (Originally published posthumously in 1925.)

Edgar Z. Friedenberg. *Coming of Age in America. Growth and Acquiescence.* New York: Random House, Inc., 1963.

N. Haan, M. B. Smith, and J. Block. "Political, Family, and Personality Correlates of Adolescent Moral Judgment." *Journal of Personality and Social Psychology,* 1968. (In press.)

H. Hartshorne and M. A. May. *Studies in the Nature of Character:* Vol. I, *Studies in Deceit.* Vol. II, *Studies in Self-Control.* Vol. III, *Studies in the Organization of Character.* New York: The Macmillan Company, 1928-30.

Nat Hentoff. *Our Children Are Dying;* and John A. McPhee. *The Headmaster: Frank L. Boyden, of Deerfield.* Two books in one volume with an introduction by Charlotte Mayerson. New York: Four Winds Press, 1966.

Philip Jackson. *Life in Classrooms.* New York: Holt, Rinehart and Winston, Inc., 1968.

Earl Kelley. *Return to Democracy.* Washington, D.C.: American Association of Elementary/Kindergarten/Nursery Educators, National Education Association, Elementary Instructional Service, 1964.

Lawrence Kohlberg. "Moral Education in the School: A Developmental View." *School Review* 74 (1): 1-30; 1966a. Revision reprinted in: Robert E. Grinder, editor. *Studies in Adolescence.* New York: The Macmillan Company, 1969. (Second Edition.)

Lawrence Kohlberg. "Moral Education, Religious Education, and the Public Schools: A Developmental View." In: Theodore Sizer, editor. *Religion and Public Education.* Boston: Houghton Mifflin Company, 1967. Chapter 8.

Lawrence Kohlberg. "The Child as a Moral Philosopher." *Psychology Today* 2 (4): 24-31; 1968.

Lawrence Kohlberg. "Education for Justice: A Modern Statement of the Platonic View." In: R. Mosher, editor. *Lectures on Moral Education.* Cambridge, Massachusetts: Harvard University Press, 1970a.

Lawrence Kohlberg. "The Concept of Moral Maturity as a Basis for Moral Education." In: E. Sullivan and B. Crittendon, editors. *Moral Development and Moral Education.* Toronto: University of Toronto Press, 1970b.

Lawrence Kohlberg. "Stage and Sequence: The Cognitive Developmental Approach to Socialization." In: D. Goslin, editor. *Handbook of Socialization Theory.* Chicago: Rand McNally & Company, 1969.

A. S. Neill. *Summerhill: A Radical Approach to Child Rearing.* New York: Hart Publishing Company, Inc. Copyright 1960.

R. S. Peters. *Ethics and Education.* Chicago: Scott, Foresman and Company, 1967.

Jean Piaget. *The Moral Judgment of the Child.* Glencoe, Illinois: The Free Press, Inc., 1948. (Originally published, 1932.)

E. Turiel. "Developmental Processes in the Child's Moral Thinking." In: P. Mussen, J. Heavenrich, and J. Langer, editors. *New Directions in Developmental Psychology.* New York: Holt, Rinehart and Winston, Inc., 1969.

Table 1. DEFINITION OF MORAL STAGES

I. PRE-CONVENTIONAL LEVEL

At this level the child is responsive to cultural rules and labels of good and bad, right or wrong, but interprets these labels in terms of either the physical or the hedonistic consequences of action (punishment, reward, exchange of favors) or in terms of the physical power of those who enunciate the rules and labels. The level is divided into the following two stages:

Stage 1: *The punishment and obedience orientation.* The physical consequences of action determine its goodness or badness regardless of the human meaning or value of these consequences. Avoidance of punishment and unquestioning deference to power are valued in their own right, not in terms of respect for an underlying moral order supported by punishment and authority (the latter being Stage 4).

Stage 2: *The instrumental relativist orientation.* Right action consists of that which instrumentally satisfies one's own needs and occasionally the needs of others. Human relations are viewed in terms like those of the marketplace. Elements of fairness, of reciprocity, and of equal sharing are present, but they are always interpreted in a physical pragmatic way. Reciprocity is a matter of "you scratch my back and I'll scratch yours," not of loyalty, gratitude, or justice.

II. CONVENTIONAL LEVEL

At this level, maintaining the expectations of the individual's family, group, or nation is perceived as valuable in its own right, regardless of immediate and obvious consequences. The attitude is not only one of *conformity* to personal expectations and social order, but of loyalty to it, of actively *maintaining*, supporting, and justifying the order and of identifying with the persons or group involved in it. At this level, there are the following two stages:

Stage 3: *The interpersonal concordance or "good boy—nice girl" orientation.* Good behavior is that which pleases or helps others and is approved by them. There is much conformity to stereotypical images of what is majority or "natural" behavior. Behavior is frequently judged by intention—"he means well" becomes important for the first time. One earns approval by being "nice."

Stage 4: *The "law and order" orientation.* There is orientation toward authority, fixed rules, and the maintenance of the social order. Right behavior consists of doing one's duty, showing respect for authority, and maintaining the given social order for its own sake.

III. Post-Conventional, Autonomous, or Principled Level

At this level, there is a clear effort to define moral values and principles which have validity and application apart from the authority of the groups or persons holding these principles and apart from the individual's own identification with these groups. This level again has two stages:

Stage 5. *The social-contract, legalistic orientation.* Generally with utilitarian overtones. Right action tends to be defined in terms of general individual rights and in terms of standards which have been critically examined and agreed upon by the whole society. There is a clear awareness of the relativism of personal values and opinions and a corresponding emphasis upon procedural rules for reaching consensus. Aside from what is constitutionally and democratically agreed upon, the right is a matter of personal "values" and "opinion." The result is an emphasis upon the "legal point of view," but with an emphasis upon the possibility of changing law in terms of rational considerations of social utility (rather than freezing it in terms of Stage 4 "law and order"). Outside the legal realm, free agreement and contract are the binding elements of obligation. This is the "official" morality of the American government and Constitution.

Stage 6: *The universal ethical principle orientation.* Right is defined by the decision of conscience in accord with self-chosen *ethical principles* appealing to logical comprehensiveness, universality, and consistency. These principles are abstract and ethical (the Golden Rule, the categorical imperative); they are not concrete moral rules like the Ten Commandments. At heart, these are universal principles of *justice,* of the *reciprocity* and *equality* of the human *rights,* and of respect for the dignity of human beings as *individual persons.*

Table 2. A Moral Dilemma and Sample Responses

In Europe, a woman was near death from a special kind of cancer. There was one drug that the doctors thought might save her. It was a form of radium that a druggist in the same town had recently discovered. The drug was expensive to make, but the druggist was charging ten times what the drug cost him to make. He paid $200 for the radium and charged $2,000 for a small dose of the drug. The sick woman's husband, Heinz, went to everyone he knew to borrow the money, but he could only get together about

$1,000, which is half of what it cost. He told the druggist that his wife was dying and asked him to sell it cheaper or let him pay later. But the druggist said, "No, I discovered the drug and I'm going to make money from it." So Heinz got desperate and broke into the man's store to steal the drug for his wife.

Should the husband have done that? Why?

MUSAMMER—AGE 10   STAGE 1   TURKISH

1. No. It's not good to steal. (Why?) If you steal some other's things one day he will steal yours, there will be a fight between the two and they will just put both in prison.

2. (Is it a husband's duty to steal the drug? Would a good husband?) No. He must go and work in order to earn the money for the drug. (If he can't?) One must give him the money. (If nobody gives?) If they don't she will die—he should not steal. (Why not?) If he steals they will put him in prison.

3. (Does the druggist have the right to charge that much for the drug if the law allows him?) No—if he charges so much from the villagemen then they won't have enough money.

4a. (If it were your wife who were dying?) I will not steal. I would let her die.

5a. If I stole they would tell on me and put me in prison—so would not.

6. They should put him in jail because he stole.

HAMZA—AGE 12   STAGE 2   TURKISH

1. Yes, because nobody would give him the drug and he had no money, because his wife was dying it was right. (Wrong not to?) Yes, because otherwise she will die.

2. (Is it a husband's duty to steal the drug?) Yes—when his wife is dying and he cannot do anything he is obliged to steal. (Why?) If he doesn't steal his wife will die.

3. (Does the druggist have the right to charge that much for the drug?) Cause he is the only store in the village it is right to sell.

4. (Should he steal the drug if he doesn't love his wife?) If he doesn't love his wife he should not steal because he doesn't care for her, doesn't care for what she says.

5. (How about if it is a good friend?) Yes—because he loves his friend and one day when he is hungry his friend would help. (If he doesn't love friend?) No—when he doesn't love him it means his friend will not help him.

6. (Should the judge punish him?) They should put him in jail because he stole.

ISKENDER—AGE 17   STAGE 4   TURKISH

1. He should not have stolen—he should have asked for the drug and they would give him the drug. (They didn't.) He should go somewhere else. (Nowhere else to go.) He should try to work for the drug. (He can't.) Then

it would be right to steal and not let his wife die because she will die and for that moment it would be right—he had to steal because his wife would die—he had to steal for the first and last time.

It is all right to steal when he can't do anything else—for the first and last time and then he should go out to work. (His duty?) It's not his duty to steal, but it is his duty to feed her.

(Did the druggist have the right to charge so much?) It's not right—laws are set up to organize people and their living—he charges so much because he is not human—if he thinks of others he must sell things so that everybody can buy.

4. (If he doesn't love her, should he steal the drug?) Because they are married he must—loving and feeling close to her has nothing to do with it. They must be together in bad or good times. Even if it's someone else who is dying he should steal. If I was in his place I would steal if I didn't know the man who was dying. He should do it only once to save somebody's life—if it's a question of death he should steal but not for anything else.

6. (Should the judge send him to jail?) It is up to the judge to decide. If he thinks the man stole just for this once and had to steal to save his wife then he would not put him in jail, but if he thinks the man will do it again and that it will become a habit then he should put him in jail. If the judge is understanding he would find a job for this man who is not working.

JAMES   STAGE 5   AMERICAN COLLEGE

Heinz did only what he had to. Had I been Heinz, I would probably have done the same thing. In any event, however, Heinz must be prepared to go to jail for breaking into a store. Breaking into the store was not "right," but the lesser of two wrongs.

(Is it his duty?) Every husband must decide which of the two wrongs—letting his wife go without the drug or stealing—is greater *to him*. I would steal.

(Did the druggist have the right to charge that much or keep the drug?) The druggist had the *right* to charge that much, although perhaps he should not have. I consider the druggist a despicable human being, even though he was acting within his rights.

RICHARD   STAGE 6   AMERICAN ADULT

(Should Heinz have done that?) Yes. It was right; human life and the right to it are prior to, and more precious than, property rights.

(Is it a husband's duty to steal the drug for his wife if he can get it no other way?) It is the husband's duty to do so. Any good husband whose ethical values were not confused would do it.

(Did the druggist have the right to charge that much when there was no law actually setting a limit to the price?) In a narrow legal sense, he had such a right. From a moral point of view, however, he had no such right.

(Heinz broke into the store and stole the drug and gave it to his wife. He was caught and brought before the judge. Should the judge send Heinz to jail for stealing, or should he let him go free? Why?) He should suspend the sentence or dismiss the charge since Heinz did no moral wrong.

Contributors

BARBARA BIBER
  Distinguished Research Scholar, Bank Street College of Education, New York

ROBERT DREEBEN
  Associate Professor of Education, University of Chicago, Illinois

EDGAR Z. FRIEDENBERG
  Professor of Sociology, State University of New York, Buffalo

JOHN D. GREENE
  ASCD President, 1970-71; Director of Instruction, Baton Rouge Public Schools, Louisiana

PHILIP W. JACKSON
  Professor of Education and Human Development, University of Chicago, Illinois

LAWRENCE KOHLBERG
  Professor of Education, Harvard University, Cambridge

PATRICIA MINUCHIN
  Associate Professor of Education, Temple University, Philadelphia

NORMAN V. OVERLY
  ASCD Associate Secretary, Washington, D.C.

ROBERT ROSENTHAL
  Professor of Social Psychology, Harvard University, Cambridge

Members of the ASCD Elementary Education Council

PHILIP W. JACKSON, *Chairman*
  Professor of Education and Human Development,
  University of Chicago, Illinois

MILDRED A. CARLSON
  Consultant in Elementary Education, Minneapolis, Minnesota

GERALD M. KNOWLES
  Assistant Professor of Education, Purdue University,
  Lafayette, Indiana

ROBERT W. LAIRD
  Education Department, The Church College of Hawaii, Laie

REBER B. LAYTON
  Director of Curriculum, Jackson, Mississippi

A. RENEE LEROY
  Coordinator, Special Projects, Pasadena City Schools,
  California

HELEN L. RICHARDS
  Head, Department of Elementary Education,
  Grambling College, Grambling, Louisiana

PHIL C. ROBINSON
  Principal, Northrup School, River Rouge, Michigan

Conference Staff

MARGARET AMMONS
   Associate Professor of Education, University of Wisconsin, Madison

MILDRED A. CARLSON
   Consultant in Elementary Education, Minneapolis, Minnesota

MAXINE DUNFEE
   Professor of Education, Indiana University, Bloomington

ROBERT GILSTRAP
   Executive Secretary, E/K/N/E—NEA, Washington, D.C.

JOHN D. GREENE
   ASCD President, 1970-71; Director of Instruction, Baton Rouge Public Schools, Louisiana

MARIE K. HAUT
   Staff Assistant, ASCD—NEA, Washington, D.C.

PHILIP W. JACKSON
   Professor of Education and Human Development, University of Chicago, Illinois

GERALD M. KNOWLES
   Assistant Professor of Education, Purdue University, Lafayette, Indiana

ROBERT W. LAIRD
   Education Department, The Church College of Hawaii, Laie

A. RENEE LeROY
   Coordinator, Special Projects, Pasadena City Schools, California

PHIL C. ROBINSON
   Principal, Northrup School, River Rouge, Michigan

ASCD Publications

(The NEA stock number appears in parentheses after each title.)

Yearbooks

Balance in the Curriculum (610-17274)	$4.00
Evaluation as Feedback and Guide (610-17700)	$6.50
Fostering Mental Health in Our Schools (610-17256)	$3.00
Guidance in the Curriculum (610-17266)	$3.75
Individualizing Instruction (610-17264)	$4.00
Leadership for Improving Instruction (610-17454)	$3.75
Learning and Mental Health in the School (610-17674)	$5.00
Learning and the Teacher (610-17270)	$3.75
Life Skills in School and Society (610-17786)	$5.50
New Insights and the Curriculum (610-17548)	$5.00
Perceiving, Behaving, Becoming: A New Focus for Education (610-17278)	$4.50
Research for Curriculum Improvement (610-17268)	$4.00
Role of Supervisor and Curriculum Director (610-17624)	$4.50
To Nurture Humaneness: Commitment for the '70's (610-17810)	$5.75
Youth Education: Problems, Perspectives, Promises (610-17746)	$5.50

Booklets

Assessing and Using Curriculum Content (611-17662)	$1.00
Better Than Rating (611-17298)	$1.25
Changing Curriculum Content (611-17600)	$1.00
The Changing Curriculum: Mathematics (611-17724)	$2.00
The Changing Curriculum: Modern Foreign Languages (611-17764)	$2.00
The Changing Curriculum: Science (611-17704)	$1.50
Changing Supervision for Changing Times (611-17802)	$2.00
Children's Social Learning (611-17326)	$1.75
Collective Negotiation in Curriculum and Instruction (611-17728)	$1.00
Criteria for Theories of Instruction (611-17756)	$2.00
Curriculum Change: Direction and Process (611-17698)	$2.00
Curriculum Decisions ⟷ Social Realities (611-17770)	$2.75
A Curriculum for Children (611-17790)	$2.75
Curriculum Materials 1970 (611-17882)	$2.00
Discipline for Today's Children and Youth (611-17314)	$1.00
Early Childhood Education Today (611-17766)	$2.00
Educating the Children of the Poor (611-17762)	$2.00
Elementary School Mathematics: A Guide to Current Research (611-17752)	$2.75
Elementary School Science: A Guide to Current Research (611-17726)	$2.25
The Elementary School We Need (611-17636)	$1.25
Extending the School Year (611-17340)	$1.25
Freeing Capacity To Learn (611-17322)	$1.00
Guidelines for Elementary Social Studies (611-17738)	$1.50
The High School We Need (611-17312)	$.50
Human Variability and Learning (611-17332)	$1.50
The Humanities and the Curriculum (611-17708)	$2.00
Humanizing Education: The Person in the Process (611-17722)	$2.25
Humanizing the Secondary School (611-17780)	$2.75
Hunters Point Redeveloped (611-17348)	$2.00
Improving Educational Assessment & An Inventory of Measures of Affective Behavior (611-17804)	$3.00
Improving Language Arts Instruction Through Research (611-17560)	$2.75
Influences in Curriculum Change (611-17730)	$2.25
Intellectual Development: Another Look (611-17618)	$1.75
The Junior High School We Need (611-17338)	$1.00
The Junior High School We Saw (611-17604)	$1.50
Juvenile Delinquency (611-17306)	$1.00
Language and Meaning (611-17696)	$2.75
Learning More About Learning (611-17310)	$1.00
Linguistics and the Classroom Teacher (611-17720)	$2.75
New Curriculum Developments (611-17664)	$1.75
New Dimensions in Learning (611-17336)	$1.50
The New Elementary School (611-17734)	$2.50
Nurturing Individual Potential (611-17606)	$1.50
Personalized Supervision (611-17680)	$1.75
Strategy for Curriculum Change (611-17666)	$1.25
Student Unrest: Threat or Promise? (611-17818)	$2.75
Supervision in Action (611-17346)	$1.25
Supervision: Emerging Profession (611-17796)	$5.00
Supervision: Perspectives and Propositions (611-17732)	$2.00
The Supervisor: Agent for Change in Teaching (611-17702)	$3.25
The Supervisor: New Demands, New Dimensions (611-17782)	$2.50
The Supervisor's Role in Negotiation (611-17798)	$.75
Theories of Instruction (611-17668)	$2.00
Toward Professional Maturity (611-17740)	$1.50
The Unstudied Curriculum: Its Impact on Children (611-17820)	$2.75
What Are the Sources of the Curriculum? (611-17522)	$1.50
Child Growth Chart (618-17442)	$.25

Discounts on quantity orders of same title to single address: 2-9 copies, 10%; 10 or more copies, 20%. Orders for $2 or less must be accompanied by remittance. Postage and handling will be charged on all orders not accompanied by payment. **The NEA stock number of each publication must be listed when ordering.**

Subscription to **Educational Leadership**—$6.50 a year. ASCD Membership dues: regular (subscription and yearbook)—$20.00 a year; Comprehensive (includes subscription and yearbook plus other publications issued during period of the membership)—$30.00 a year.

Order from: **Association for Supervision and Curriculum Development, NEA**
1201 Sixteenth Street, N.W.   Washington, D.C. 20036